Unlocking the Moviemaking Mind

Tales of Voice, Vision, and Video from K-12 Classrooms

Michael Schoonmaker and John M. Wolf

ROWMAN & LITTLEFIELD EDUCATION
A division of
ROWMAN & LITTLEFIELD
Lanham • Boulder • New York • Toronto • Plymouth, UK

Published by Rowman & Littlefield Education
A division of Rowman & Littlefield
4501 Forbes Boulevard, Suite 200, Lanham, Maryland 20706
www.rowman.com

10 Thornbury Road, Plymouth PL6 7PP, United Kingdom

British Library Cataloguing in Publication Information Available

Library of Congress Cataloging-in-Publication Data

Library of Congress Cataloging-in-Publication Data Available
ISBN 978-1-4758-0388-4 (cloth : alk. paper) -- ISBN 978-1-4758-0389-1 (pbk. : alk. paper) -- ISBN
978-1-4758-0390-7 (electronic)

∞™ The paper used in this publication meets the minimum requirements of American
National Standard for Information Sciences Permanence of Paper for Printed Library
Materials, ANSI/NISO Z39.48-1992.

Printed in the United States of America

Contents

Preface

By Michael Schoonmaker

Unlocking the Moviemaking Mind is an unfolding narrative about the growing potential of video production in K-12 classrooms. It is designed as a thought-provoking roadmap for teachers of all K-12 subjects who want to find effective and engaging ways to invigorate their twenty-first century lesson plans. It is written for teachers who have witnessed the natural fascination kids have for mediamaking and shares insights from a rapidly expanding population of K-12 teachers around the country and world who have already tapped into the power of visual expression in their classrooms.

The book explores both the known and not-so-known frontier of K-12. Videomaking is designed to equip teachers to meet their unique challenges and objectives, in their own ways. Findings are derived from a wide spectrum of activities over the past five years, including:

- Updates to and reconsiderations of ideas from my book *Cameras in the Classroom* (2007). In this book I confronted the strange anomaly that nearly all kids entering school are fully functional readers of visual media, yet K-12 curricula were still hesitant to fully embrace visual media in learning environments. On top of this, "visually-ready" students were trapped in a holding pattern in terms of their lack of access to the tools of visual expression. They can "read" the visual media of others, but they are short of the necessary tools and skills to "write" their own visual expressions. Since then, there has been a slow but sure move on teachers' parts to correct this educational incongruity.
- Test-flown perspectives first presented in my online column in *School Video News*. The column was designed to help K-12 educators expand and improve the use of visual media in classrooms across the nation. The teachers and students I came to know through this experience added exponentially to my knowledge base.
- Fresh findings straight from middle school classrooms: "The Smart Kids Visual Stories Project" — a three-year study of the role of visual media in giving voice to the voiceless: stories, insights, and ideas for reform from students in an urban public school district.

- Collaboration with my colleague John Wolf who has worked with me in many of the above endeavors and brings to this book a deep understanding of the convergence of humanity and technology, along with his true gift in finding order, however small it may be, in chaos of all shapes and sizes.

And a final thought: Studying young moviemakers has certainly taught us how kids can use visual expression to enhance learning. But it has also helped us understand how deeply entwined humanity and visual expression are at the heart of any moviemaking experience, be it professional, educational, or recreational. There is a child within every moviemaker, and a moviemaker within every child.

Introduction: Journey to Video Production in K-12

The undocumented life is not worth living. This sentiment—whether you agree with it, take issue with it, or just smirk at the Socratic reference—hyperbolic though it may be, is a good reflection of participatory culture at the beginning of the 21st century. As information and communication technologies like smartphones, digital video cameras, and user-generated content sites like YouTube continue to evolve at a rapid pace, we're presented with further opportunities to document our lives, share our lived experiences, and actively participate in digital storytelling.

Throughout this book we explore the possibilities for digital storytelling in the K-12 classroom. The findings are based on a multi-year research project that examined the outcomes and effects of digital storytelling in urban, public schools. Narratives from these experiences are organized thematically and presented in a three-part structure. Each part is composed of numerous chapters as well as interludes that serve to synthesize and contextualize important information, ideas, and theories presented throughout the book.

Although this book tells a liner narrative from beginning to end, it isn't necessary to read it linearly. Each part (described below) offers a unique set of useful ideas and stories, so feel free to plan your journey to suit your own needs or to jump around from one part of the book to another.

WHY ARE YOU HERE?

Maybe you're an educator who's interested in somehow incorporating video production into your lesson plans. Maybe you're an administrator who wants to encourage her teachers to engage in classroom-based media production exercises. Maybe you're a graduate student who has an investment in constructionist, hands-on education. Maybe you're a scholar who's surveying the current literature on the use of contemporary technologies in the classroom. Or maybe you just liked the cover of this book and thought the title sounded cool.

Regardless as to why you're here: Welcome. This book is written from the point of view of two educators who have spent years thinking about, writing about, and researching digital media production in the K-12 classroom. This book is written for anyone with an interest in this subject. Educators will find useful information and convincing evidence for making the leap to using video production in the classroom. Similarly, educators who have already integrated video production into their curricula will discover useful philosophies as well as practical applications for refining their techniques. Students and scholars can indulge in findings from experimental research pertaining to storytelling, participatory culture, and media studies. And those simply with an interest in the subject will discover a tale of untapped potential, unlikely hope, and creative ingenuity.

The prospect of introducing video production in the K-12 classroom can seem daunting at first. You may find that your mind is overwhelmed with questions at the very thought of it. What does it take to produce a video? What if I lack familiarity with the necessary technologies/vocabulary/skillsets? What makes a good video? What learning outcomes can video production help my students achieve? What if the school doesn't have the budget/funds/infrastructure to support such an endeavor? And countless other ones, no doubt.

While it is true that there are a great number of practical, institutional, and systematic hurdles to overcome in introducing video production in the K-12 classroom, there is an equal, if not greater, amount of something else that makes the endeavor worth the wager: Possibility. In short, video production in the K-12 classroom works. Students engaged in video production interventions display gains in self-esteem, self-efficacy, self-possession, and critical thinking. Students who are more confident are more likely to believe they can successfully undertake assigned tasks and, thus, fare better in school.

While we know from research and experience that video production interventions work in K-12 classrooms when executed properly, we don't necessarily know why. Using data collected from several years of fieldwork, Part I explores why video production seems to work so well in the K-12 classroom. We begin by investigating storytelling as the core of video production and exploring the relationship between storytelling and the human condition. We then lay out some important considerations for successfully implementing digital video production in the classroom. Finally, we present some tried and true methods and ideas for introducing students to video production as an educational resource.

Part II presents evidence as to how digital video production can be used in the K-12 classroom to overcome those individual and systematic challenges and barriers common to public education. First we investigate the relationships between video production, self-discovery, and motivation. Next we explore video production as a metaphor for voice and what it means for students to be able to articulate agency, to be heard rather than merely listened to, and to knowingly share meaningful parts of their existences with others.

While Part I offers tried and true strategies and Part II considers uses of video production to overcome institutional challenges, Part III offers some abstract ideas and considerations for successfully implementing digital video strategies in the K-12 classroom. These ideas are not merely academic; rather, they speak to a necessary mindset that educators should adopt when thinking about incorporating video production into their classrooms. We consider the possibility of thinking about video as a new type of literacy, proposing a radical reinterpretation of the traditional understanding of what it means to be able to read and write. Finally, we examine video production in the classroom as a dimension of human engagement that is sometimes necessarily uncomfortable and messy, encouraging educators and practitioners to pay equal attention to process and outcome.

Part One

Keys

Telling Stories and Storytelling

It's all about story. Or, more specifically, it's all about *storytelling*: an effortful or automatic cognitive sense-making process in which we arrange, organize, and present a series of events that are reflective of our thoughts, perceptions, and life experiences.

Storytelling can be classified as effortful, automatic, or some combination of both. *Effortful storytelling* involves explicitly engaging in storytelling practices. Examples of effortful storytelling include creating stories intended for entertainment (TV shows, films, novels, etc.) or to teach a lesson (folklore, fairy tales, fables, etc.). Effortful storytelling may be thought of as classic storytelling, the kind in which we consciously choose to engage. There are defined times and spaces for effortful storytelling (bedtime, primetime, Friday nights, etc.), and, by and large, it is the type of storytelling that we will focus on throughout this book.

However, there is another type of storytelling in which we often engage that we also consider throughout this book. When compared to effortful storytelling, this type of storytelling is less obvious and the process by which we engage in it is often less conscious. On account of these facts, we may be less inclined to think of it as storytelling; it is, nonetheless, classifiable as a type of storytelling, and although it seems to exist apart from effortful storytelling, it does not. In fact, this type of storytelling borrows heavily on our understanding of story as it is informed by effortful storytelling. This kind of storytelling is called automatic storytelling.

Automatic storytelling is the kind of storytelling in which we are engaged throughout the day. Stories that result from this kind of storytelling are fundamental to the ways in which we describe, characterize, and understand ourselves, others, and the world around us. We commonly don't think of them as stories; rather, we're more likely to label them beliefs, facts, or truths. Although less clearly discernable as a type of storytelling, this practice is arguably more important in stressing the inherent link between our humanity and storytelling.

To demonstrate this point, consider the following statement: I am white. On one hand, this statement is a mere classification of my race, which is a reflection of my skin color. On account of the fact that we are innately social creatures, however, this statement conveys a multitude of information beyond just skin color. To identify as white is to claim a certain social standing and degree of privilege. To identify as white is to claim a shared history and collective experience with other white people. To identify as white is to claim familiarity with specific cultural norms, mores, and institutions. To identify as white (or any other identity marker, for that matter) is to tell a story about yourself to yourself and to others.

Stories that result from automatic storytelling are identity affirming insofar as they tell a story that allows individuals to make sense of their place in the world. Furthermore, these stories provide insight as to how individuals are likely to make sense of others who claim a specific identity trait. That these stories are arbitrary—meaning that they are informed by such factors as time, place, and subjective experience—matters little; they affect social reality because they are popular enough so that, in general, people believe them.

Thus, effortful or automatic, we are always engaged in some form of storytelling, whether we are retelling an old story, learning a new one, or questioning the truth of the ones we've been told. In this way, we can think of storytelling as a fundamental component of our humanity. In the following chapters, we begin to explore the nature and origin of stories, specifically in the context of doing video production to the K-12 classroom.

ONE
Instinct

The reason why so many people are opting out of education is because it doesn't feed their spirit. . . . We have to go from what is essentially an industrial model of education, a manufacturing model, which is based on linearity, and conformity and batching people. . . . We have to recognize that human flourishing is not a mechanical process, it's an organic process. . . . All you can do, like a farmer, is to create the conditions under which they will begin to flourish.
—Sir Ken Robinson, International Advisor on Education[1]

Whenever we ask our college filmmaking students to quantify how many movies they have in their heads, they get excited as they contemplate the number, because there are so very many. When we first asked K-12 students (all different grade levels), it surprised us when they responded exactly the same way.

It was surprising because we had always thought such a trait was more likely to be a sign of a person's vocational attraction to the practice of filmmaking. But as we've come to find time and time again, thinking in moving pictures is actually more of a universal human quality than a specialized one. And recent developments in neuroscience (Gazzaniga, 2012) have confirmed studio-like story factory our minds are capable of building.

In his article "The 'Interpreter' in Your Head Spins Stories to Make Sense of the World," brain researcher Michael Gazziniga explains, "This is what our brain does all day long. It takes input from other areas of our brain and from the environment and synthesizes it into a story." In this light, the human mind could be seen as an organic moviemaking machine.

We recently had an opportunity to see this "moviemaking machine" in full gear when we asked a group of middle school students to create

5

visual stories about their school experiences. In most cases, the visual story process began with extensive conversations. We asked kids about what they wanted to tell stories about and since as a rule they had so many stories to tell, as opposed to just one, our challenge was to help them narrow down their many stories to the one they felt most important to share. This process involved many sessions and many conversations before single stories were arrived at.

During one of our school visits, later in the story development process, four kids asked if they could join in the already-underway story project. We agreed to include them, and since time was of the essence—it was time to finish the stories as opposed to starting them at this point in the project—we asked them to be part of a storytelling experiment. Instead of having multiple sessions of conversation-based story development, we wanted to see if we could actually "extract" a movie that was already in their head.

One of the latecomers, Aadila, quickly volunteered. The question we posed to her was, "Children have told us that they have all kinds of movies in their head. These stories are about everything in their lives. Do you have movies like this in your mind?"

"Yes," she replied without hesitation.

"Could you please share the essence of one of those movies in your head that is about school? Even if you have a hundred stories about school, share the first one that comes to mind and don't worry whether it's right or wrong or good or bad, just tell us what it is."

For one, slow motion moment, Aadila's wide eyes looked upward in the direction of some distant dream and then returned. She proceeded to tell us a long and vivid account about how the daily antics of her fellow seventh graders were so destructive in the school environment. They almost always started with some sort of Facebook incident, then confrontations in classrooms, fights (what she termed the "free admission entertainment"), and some unexplainable, instant and infuriating reconciliation. Yes, this was an everyday occurrence at her middle school and it came down to one word: drama.

What was surprising about Aadila's response was not just how instant it was. It was over in a matter of thirty seconds, it was very "logistically doable" as a visual story, and the kids who witnessed it wanted in. What was also surprising was how rich and interesting the story was, easily comparable to stories that had taken days and even weeks to develop with other story groups. It's certainly possible that we just got lucky with Aadila's first movie. But the more we've thought about it since finishing the story titled "Drama," the more we've seen this experiment as a bellwether of innate student capabilities and natural resources.

Tools

Though videomaking is technically *not* organic—it is a technological process—it has a strong association with the very organic practice of storytelling. Human beings, young and old, are hardwired to tell stories, and video cameras give them a rich visual resource to do so.

Video cameras are certainly not the only tools of organic learning that learners have at their disposal. Videomaking is one of many educational technologies that can be harnessed for organic learning, or as Robinson framed it, conditions for human flourishing. The computer, along with the world of applications and online accompaniments, offers the same conduit to organic learning with a camera. Interestingly neither of these tools can make use of organic learning in and of themselves.

The recent failure of the British ICT curriculum—the Information and Communication Technologies component that guides educators on standards in teaching technology and communications—curriculum in Britain demonstrates precisely this point. This top-down introduction to basic computer skills and technology failed because of its near complete disconnection to the root of the learning process: the learner. UK Education Secretary Michael Gove[2] explained the problem wasn't the technology, but rather how it was being used in the classroom:

> By withdrawing the Programme of Study, we're giving teachers freedom over what and how to teach, revolutionising ICT as we know it. . . . By withdrawing the Programme of Study, we're giving teachers freedom over what and how to teach, revolutionizing ICT as we know it. . . . Instead of children bored out of their minds being taught how to use Word and Excel by bored teachers, we could have 11-year-olds able to write simple 2D computer animations. . . . By 16, they could have an understanding of formal logic previously covered only in University courses and be writing their own Apps for smartphones.

This bottom up realization on Grove's and the UK's part raises another very important question about organic learning environments: At what point in the learning process should the learners be introduced to the tools of learning?

Sooner Is Better

The reality is that when it comes to technology, children are ready to engage, should we allow them to, very early on in their development—certainly at the beginning of their formal education. Though by no means technology experts, as many digital immigrants might nervously claim, they are ripe for real and deep learning, not unlike the way they interact with everything from toys to language. For instance if you put a very young child (2 or 3 years old) in front of a computer, they will not only learn how to use it with surprisingly little prompting, but they will also use it to learn more.

This incredible tendency has both excited and infuriated educators like Anthony Lorenzo. Anthony was a fourth grade teacher and ICT Co-ordinator for two schools in the Tuscany region of Northern Italy. What struck us immediately upon meeting him was his continually flowing energy and ideas when it came to the challenges of education. We didn't have much time to work with him before his long teaching day would take him away, so we talked fast and got to know each other very quickly.

The moment we walked into his classroom, the principal of the school notified him that the school's server had crashed on one of the most important days of the school year. Anthony apologized almost at the same moment that he deftly vanished and restored the server, after which our conversations continued.

He was clearly a passionate teacher with an open mind and un-quenchable curiosity. Beyond the incredible romantic facade of his two "storybook" campuses, Anthony faced the same challenges and valued the same outcomes of teachers we have talked with across the United States. Looking at those challenges, like archaic school systems, and those desired outcomes, like the goal to inspire lifelong learning in children, from the other side of the ocean gave poignant clarity to the organic opportunity to connect with twenty-first-century learners. Ironically we were seeing it as plain as day in an environment more often associated with the fourteenth-century Renaissance.

It was difficult to contain our videomaking sensations as this "com-puter guy" demonstrated on a small table in the school's art studio— windows overlooking winding vineyards, rolling hillsides, terracotta rooftops, and the unmistakable aura of the distant *duomo*—a prototype of a 3D interactive art display utilizing Wii game hardware and free soft-ware available on the web.

What continually infuriated Anthony, in stark contrast to the exciting technological possibilities of the twenty-first-century world, was that he had all kinds of ideas about computer and media literacy, but not enough opportunities to apply them to the numbers of people who would benefit from them. "If I could just have them, for even a short amount of time," he implored, "I know I could give students these essential lessons about computers and computing to empower them for the rest of their lives. It doesn't have to be much!"

The trouble was, on both sides of the Atlantic—and especially in the higher grades—finding that extra time in an already stacked curriculum weighed down by so many other mandates is challenging, if not impos-sible. If only there was a way to get those technological tools of learning to them earlier in their educational development, say in Kindergarten where they have the time to "play." This would require a revolution of sorts to what has always been a delicate and fragile process of introducing young learners to the process of education.

Seeds of Learning

In another unlikely corner of the world, educational scientist Sugata Mitra[3] illustrated the possibilities engaging very young learners in a fascinating experiment he called "Hole in the Wall."

Mitra placed computer kiosks in slum areas and watched as children found and eventually mastered—with no assistance whatsoever, a term Mitra coined "minimally invasive learning"—the technology and used it for their own learning needs. What this experiment demonstrated is how simple human curiosity can ignite learning when the proper tools are provided.

To work in an educational setting, any teaching tool or technology depends upon a larger organic force. In the case of video production in the classroom, that force is composed of our innate tendency to tell stories, our curiosity, and the instinct to learn.

NOTES

1. Filmed presentation at *Ted Talks*, February 2010, titled *Bring on the learning revolution!* See http://www.ted.com/talks/sir_ken_robinson_bring_on_the_revolution.html.

2. http://www.education.gov.uk/inthenews/inthenews/a00201864/harmful-ict-curriculum-set-to-be-dropped-this-september-to-make-way-for-rigorous-computer-science.

3. See *Hole in the Wall* on Mitra's website. http://www.hole-in-the-wall.com/contactus.aspx.

TWO

Connection

There is a consistent question rising up from the latest work we have done with K-12 students using video cameras in their classes: Which came first: Hollywood or the mind's eye? In other words does the culture of being raised in a world filled with movies and TV shows inform and structure our thought process, or is Hollywood derived from the inner Cineplex we are born with in our heads?

This is one of those chicken-and-the-egg questions, complete with the initial commonsensical trap, "Of course it had to be the egg (the mind's eye) because how could you have the chicken (Hollywood) without first having an egg?" The question also has a chicken-first answer.

The Chicken Answer

If you ask a college-age filmmaking student how many movies they have in their head, they can't usually put a specific number on the notion, but they do admit there are a lot—maybe hundreds—and they delight in the idea of one day sharing them all with others.

The problem with all these movies in their heads is that there is no easy way to get them out, at least when it comes to conventional film and television production practices. Filmmaking is one of those things in life that looks so easy to do, mostly because we can effortlessly watch these works as audiences of them, but in reality it is extremely difficult.

When freshman filmmakers screen their very first works they are often embarrassed. It's liberating for them to show the films, but they are rarely satisfied with what they see on the screen. The problem is that their idea of their film was so clear and beautiful in their head, but something got lost in the translation from their head to the screen. It's not that they're dumb or incapable of being successful filmmakers. It's just very difficult to do and takes a few drafts to make presentable.

What would it be like if these students could magically monitor that special place in the brain where their visual imagination resides and directly project their inner movies on a screen for everyone else to see? There would be no need for cameras, lighting, microphones, or even scripts. Their movie stories would all be right at their fingertips, flowing, revealing, and clear.

But without such a miracle monitor, most of what we do in the movie-making process is a clumsy attempt to replicate the mind's eye by *re-presenting* our stories on the screen in much the same manner that our imaginations project them in our brain tissue, complete with the illusion of visual and aural perception, point of view, focus, and perhaps most importantly: meaning.

When asked the "Which came first?" question, young filmmakers might be inclined to lean toward Hollywood, given their recent discovery of how difficult and unnatural it is to transform their personal narratives to the screen. The mind's eye may be something they were born with, but a Hollywood eye, along with the tremendously complicated encoding process it involves, must be learned. Their newly found filmmaking skills, and its expanded critical awareness, also tend to mature and reshape their thought process. For instance, now when they contemplate a future movie project in their mind's eye, it may include a lighting plan and structural story device.

These students are focused on becoming publicly acclaimed filmmakers and TV producers, and they hold a certain reverence for mysteries behind making it big in the motion picture industries. There is nothing natural or intuitive about the filmmaking project akin to how easy it is to flip on one's visual imagination. And they take pride in their newly acquired skills.

The Egg Answer

However, when it comes to the fourth, fifth, and sixth graders we work with, the equation leans the other way. These youngsters seem more comfortable in their organic interactions with the camera and editing gear. They, and we, are not focused on emulating Oscar and Emmy worthy professional practices and story strategies (though their works are beautiful in other ways). Rather we are enjoying the novelty (compared to other classroom activities) and kinetic qualities of the media-making experience. And the object of the research we are doing with them is to encourage them to express themselves in ways related to their particular learning objectives. The overall experience feels more like a game than work, and a very natural and engaging game at that.

When we're on our way out of the schools we work in, we can't help feeling a real excitement about where we are going with these kids and their video cameras. Part of it is the sheer energy involved in exploring the expressive delights of the children. Another part is watching the joy and creativity in their expressions that pour out like water from a faucet stuck wide open.

When you think about it, we might be closer to that magic monitoring device in the brain when we tap the visual expressions of untrained, unrefined, unconditioned, pure moviemakers than we are when we watch polished works of their heavily trained, experienced, comparatively mature and professionally focused counterparts. Why is this?

One reason might be that the further we get from professional movie-making practice, the closer we get to the genuine selves of young moviemakers. Current research in neuroscience (Gazzaniga, 2012) is also leaning in this direction, suggesting that if there is such a thing as a command center for the human brain, it seems to be closely connected with the natural human tendency to make sense of their worlds through storytelling. In Gazzinga's research, it is the story that we tell ourselves in our inner monologue that creates the illusion of consciousness we experience as living, breathing "selves." He writes (Gazzaniga, 2012), "Our subjective awareness arises out of our dominant left hemisphere's unrelenting quest to explain the bits and pieces that pop into consciousness."

In educational terms, storytelling could be seen as an outward exercise of this natural, internal process of sense-making, and it does not seem a far-fetched possibility that we could connect this storytelling process to classroom activities and objectives.

In addition, when we try to monitor, connect with, and share the movies in our mind, we thus could be seen to be engaging in a natural process, square at the core of who we are, as opposed to a highly technical process which moviemaking is most often understood to be.

Thinking about my college film students grimacing in the screen's reflection of their first cuts, it would stand to reason that there is nothing inherently natural when it comes to the framing of their stories through a professional moviemaking process, for little of their story comes out as easily as they imagined it. And the professionally rooted moviemaking practices I am teaching them are serving only to aggravate any honest and untainted connection between their minds and a camera.

When we play video camera games with elementary school kids, we seem to be genuinely closer to their untainted stories, their inner selves, and the actual movies in their minds. The camera exercise is not as much a process of translation and extraction for formal public presentation; rather, it is an honest and visually rough expression. But to appreciate these kinds of formless, unstructured stories, we likely need to watch them differently and learn to recognize substance amidst chaos, what Virginia Woolf would have termed "a pattern behind the cotton wool." Near the end of her life she wrote about the story-like fabric of the human condition:

> ... it is a constant idea of mine; that behind the cotton wool is hidden a pattern; that we—I mean all human beings—are connected with this; that the whole world is a work of art; that we are parts of the work of art; that we are all parts of a work of art. *Hamlet* or a Beethoven quartet is the truth about this vast mass that we call the world. But there is no Shakespeare, there is no Beethoven; certainly and empathetically there is no God; we are the words; we are the music; we are the thing itself.
>
> —Virginia Woolf (1925)

Likewise, you could say, there is great potential (educational and otherwise) in connecting the movies in our minds with others.

THREE
Nature

On the surface, the college-level video/TV production culture might appear very different than the K-12 brand. For instance, the typical student in my production classes is a well-rounded, focused, driven, and high performing individual who sees him- or herself in a professional position in the media industry immediately after graduation. They are, in short, very serious about media and their professional future in it. Because these students share so much in their ability and aspirations, the professional approach to teaching them production (including media tools and resources I call upon) is similarly focused and consistent.

The K-12 video/TV production scene is much more complicated by comparison. Students not only *come from* very different places in terms of their interests and abilities, but they are also *headed to* very different places. The approach to media activities with such a diverse group is similarly complicated.

At the root level, however, more similarities emerge. One thing that seems to unite these two groups is the visible satisfaction students exhibit in sharing their media creations with other people. We often talk about this with our college students telling them it's something we moviemakers share in our DNA. We have the *storytelling gene*.

This explanation results in a glimmer of familiarity and acceptance. They nod in agreement, as if some secret behind their intense motivations has been revealed. On the very simplest of levels, people with this media-making DNA strand care profoundly about what other people think and feel, and they want to engage these other people in some way.

Sharing our visions gives us purpose. It certainly seems to ignite self-esteem. But within this need to share lies a significant challenge to media-makers: the challenge of having something to say. The actual technology, work, and craftsmanship of media-making, however time consuming

15

and backbreaking it might be, is much easier in comparison to the challenges of having something to say.

For instance, we explain to students that a filmmaker is the metaphorical equivalent of a spot-lit figure standing up on stage in front of a large audience waiting for this storyteller at the podium to give them something they don't already have. What does the storyteller do now? Hopefully, what they have to share will be a worthwhile and fulfilling experience for the audience. Having something meaningful to say is by far the greatest challenge to a media-maker.

The best we can hope for as media-makers is that our audience will leave feeling moved by our works. Filmmaking students often talk about their dreams of making someone else feel as good as they felt after watching a great movie. They want to give back. Having something to say when it's time to share our stories, and truly "giving back," are not arbitrary acts of pointing the video camera at whatever is in front of us. These aspirations involve connecting the camera to the purpose, vision, and creativity within us, and articulating these elements aurally and visually for others to appreciate. The value in this for an audience is in experiencing perspectives from points of view other than their own.

Whether a media-maker is creating content for a professional studio or television network or their social studies teacher, they are fueled by their hope and desire to impress those who read or listen or watch or click on that content—including their bosses and teachers.

For filmmaking students, the object of their efforts is an unseen, and unforgiving, public. If they are successful they receive increasing compensation and public recognition for their efforts. The object of K-12 student efforts is a little different: teachers, parents, and peers. If they are successful, they receive an academic reward, compliments, a boost in self-esteem, but perhaps more important than all of that, they receive a meaningful and lasting education. In visually and aurally playing out their subject matter and ideas in their own way, students can cross the line between learning and living—applying learning to their own expression, all fueled by their intense desire to share—their media-making DNA.

With this in mind, it seems a bit ridiculous to characterize media makers as genetically different than other humans. Is it out of the realm of possibility that being seen and recognized in a positive way is closer to a universally human trait and desire? If so, then why wouldn't media-making be considered a partner in the learning process, or more fittingly, the DNA of an inquiring mind?

In the end, it's not the "DNA factor" that distinguishes media-making professionals (or professionals-in-training) from others. It's more the way that "DNA" is used. In the professional's case, it is skill-driven, toward industry success. In the student's case it is lesson-driven, toward educational success.

It is gratifying as a filmmaking teacher to talk to others about what we do: we teach a highly captive audience—captive to the love of expressing their ideas to others. The reaction from those we brag to is predictable: "That seems like it must be fun to do." And it certainly is a true joy to teach students something they want to learn. When we consider why they love this "moviemaking thing," it's easy to characterize it as a specialty interest, like a DNA trait.

But considering the same question in realm of K-12 media-making, the answer gets more interesting. It never ceases to amaze us how much K-12 students enjoy the experience of making videos, even when they learn that it involves a lot of time commitment and real work. In the end, it's clear that the love of visual storytelling is not all that unique. It is more broadly human nature to enjoy the act of sharing stories and impacting an audience.

FOUR

Motivation

If there has been one finding more resonant than all others over years of K-12 videomaking (Schoonmaker, 2007), it is something we call the *relevance factor*. By relevance we are referring to an inherent comfort, understanding, and buy-in on students' parts when it comes to educational activities. There is purpose in their learning when video is involved.

What we have consistently found is that videomaking seems to make the educational activities associated with it more relevant to young learners than they would have through more traditional instructional means of exposure, such as teacher-to-student lecturing, use of written handouts, film strips, videos, audio recordings and field trips, and even the simple act of writing terms and concepts on a black or white board.

The Idea of Relevance

The learning process comes with a question on students' parts about why they are doing what they are doing: a continual, "What's the point of this?" By necessity then, teachers are involved in a process of engaging their audiences. For a lesson to take complete hold on a learner, it must be relevant to the learner. To the extent that they can, teachers must communicate some sense of why it is important for students to learn a particular topic or lesson while they are learning it. But, there is not always time or opportunity to do this within the day-to-day milieu of school.

The principle of relevance is not too far afloat from a similarly in-built aspect of the moviemaking process: *suspension of disbelief* (Schoonmaker, 2007). Suspension of disbelief is a term to describe the depth of involvement a viewer is willing to give to a fictional story. When they sit down to watch a movie, audience members go through a superficial stage of story engagement.

19

First, they take in basic story information and consider whether the story is worth experiencing or entering. Even though they have made a preliminary decision to consider the story, there still is time to gather information on whether it is the kind of story they might find interesting, or not. They can always walk out of the movie theater or change the channel, depending on how well this preliminary stage of the process goes.

In this stage they ask, "Is the story believable?" or "Is it a complete blatantly sloppy fabrication?" Believable stories are preferred as a rule because we usually prefer to surrender our imaginations to the story and let it take us away as viewers.

Storytellers must therefore prepare their stories for such viewer demands. Even though the suspension of belief factor is ancillary to the story, effectively achieving it is vital to the overall success of the story. This usually means we have to get to the point of the story quickly, usually by beginning with some sort of action. Action encourages participation in the story, because it moves like our lives. And our stories and characters have to be believable and authentic if viewers are going to relate to them as if they were real people.

If a story can maintain consistent plausibility throughout and viewers are sufficiently engaged as they seek information and authenticity in it, then we can expect that they will suspend their disbelief in the artificial act of, among other things, watching a story unfold on a clearly artificial screen and they will join in the story experience as if it was an event in their lives.

The idea of relevance in educational environments is very similar. The more realistically plausible a lesson is to the future of the learner—in other words they see value and relevance as it relates to their future lives—the more likely the lesson will be successful all-round.

Relevance in Practice

We saw the relevance factor in action in many different ways at all levels of K-12: field trips, class behavior demonstrations, history lessons, and other challenging academic subjects like research and poetry. Regardless of the subject, the effect was the same: A video camera gave a license of relevance to subject matters it was connected to. The question we continue to wrestle with is why is this case?

Novelty.   To some degree, it might be the novelty of a camera in a classroom environment. Though video cameras are not yet the rule in K-12 environments, they are more common than they used to be given the proliferation and democratization of the digital technology. For instance, every child that has a phone has a video camera in his or her pocket. But most teachers have not found regular, easy, or effective ways to involve cameras in their lesson plans, opting for more familiar and comparatively "safe" traditional means of instruction. So when a camera is brought into a classroom it still can be considered a novelty of sorts. Novelty breeds curiosity, and curiosity breeds the opportunity for relevance: if I am curious, I want to know something and if that something is in the direction of a lesson plan I will seek it out of curiosity.

If the relevance of a video camera and its visual insights is truly and only a novelty, then it can be expected to last at least until the next novelty arrives to take its place.

Kinetics. But there is the chance that the relevance factor is fueled by something else as well: the action—call it kinetics—of the production process.

> I hear and I forget.
> I see and I remember.
> I do and I understand.
> —Confucius

Videomaking has a strong kinetic quality to it from the physical activity of operating it to the fairly laborious process of conceiving it. It also adds kinetic quality to its subject matter, by incorporating moving image media into a topic. A video, like a paper, is idea driven and when that idea is connected to a lesson plan, it adds kinetic energy to it. With kinetic energy comes the opportunity for relevance.

Familiarity. One other aspect behind videomaking's tendency to bring relevance to subject matters it is associated with is its familiarity. Children born in the past four or five decades basically grow up with moving image media all around them from birth. It is a familiar, thus relevant, part of the world they know and live in. Children learn to "read" television in their infancy, and arrive to kindergarten visually literate in terms of television watching. When they learn the alphabet, they are gaining a comparatively new literacy in print media.

But most classrooms current K-12 students reside in are not equipped with or outfitted for the free and easy use of visual media. Some of this has to do with the fact that school districts do not have unlimited resources and must make hard choices about what they can and cannot equip classrooms with. Another part of it has to do with technological inertia and the fact that teachers are not prepared to deal with additional media resources. Teachers are more skilled and comfortable with traditional learning resources and relatively slow to adapt to new ways of teaching that involve unfamiliar tools, such as video cameras. There is also a psychological resistance of sorts when it comes to the comfort level of teachers using popular media like television and film (let alone cameras) because of residual skepticism in the educational community concerning the use of popular media forms in the classroom.

So, when cameras occasionally appear in these environments they look more like environments outside of classrooms and are therefore more relevant to the world children know outside of their classrooms.

Classroom Case Studies in Relevance: Football

Videomaking is certainly not the only relevant element in K-12 students' lives, and we often witnessed examples of good teachers exploring the challenge of relevance in innovative ways. We were actually working with students on a video project when something even more relevant than the videomaking activity we were involved in drew them away from their filmmaking: football.

Sixth graders Ronnie and Tyrone were brainstorming ideas for a visual story about their school when a football game began out on the playground, which was tantalizingly visible from the window of the room we were working in. As the distraction of the game drew them further away from the task at hand, it was easy to fall prey to the instinct to bring them back to the table. But there was something about the way that they politely pleaded to take a break from our creative brainstorming that we couldn't resist. Maybe it was the fact that it was so rare when something competed with their attention and involvement with videomaking activities that made us curious. So we compromised and brought the video cameras outside to record the game. Little did we know that we were not taking a break—we were beginning production of their video story.

It turns out that their teacher, Katie DiLorenzo, regularly rewarded her students with a football game on the playground when they earned it in the classroom. She was the designated quarterback (dress, heels, and all) for both sides and involved every member of the class in the activity regardless of their knowledge of or ability in the game of football. As we talked to Ronnie and Tyrone on the sidelines about how to cover the action of a football game with two cameras, it became clear that this activity was not about the sport of football. It was about being in school and learning.

Kate DiLorenzo taught a broad range of subjects in her sixth grade class, but she situated them within the context of sportsmanship and competition. She was a quarterback in the class as much as on the field and she used the relevance factor of team sports to enliven and enrich her lesson plans.

Ronnie and Tyrone considered Ms. DiLorenzo a model of a good teacher. It was at that point that they decided that this was the story they wanted to tell about what it was like to be a student in an urban school: What a good teacher looks like. In the simplest of terms it was her mastery of motivating her students by connecting lesson plans to an everyday part of the world her students understood. In the boys' words, it was football.

Video beyond Vocation

Introducing media creation projects in the K-12 classroom seems to work for two separate, though related, reasons:

First, these types of exercises exploit our innate capacity as storytellers. The previous chapters have highlighted the many ways in which storytelling is fundamental to our humanity and, furthermore, how this essential quality can be put to work in the K-12 classroom.

Second, they are highly relevant to many, if not all, contemporary learners. And relevance, in this case, is multifaceted. Not only are contemporary learners likely to be highly interested in—and, thus, motivated by—these types of projects, they are also likely to arrive in the classroom with many of the necessary skills and technological acumen already in place.

So far, we've discussed why video is successful in the K-12 classroom. At this point you may be convinced of the likelihood of video projects to engage students, but you may find yourself wondering how video can be successfully deployed in the classroom. Thus, we now turn our attention to some strategies for success in using video in the classroom.

Perhaps one of the most important points to understand about the use of video production in the K-12 classroom is that video—in this context, at least—is *not* vocation. One of the biggest misconceptions about introducing video production in the K-12 classroom is that the teacher must have prior experience or expertise in this area. This is not the case; there are no prerequisites. While educators should become familiar with some basic terms, expressions, and concepts prior to introducing video production in the classroom, the technology itself is secondary to the planned learning outcomes of the lesson.

In order to be successful with video in the classroom, students need support, encouragement, and, perhaps most importantly, direction. Using video in the classroom will undoubtedly be exciting for students, but the acquisition and mastery of video production skills is not the primary focus of video production in this context; rather, video production should be regarded as simply another means for students to express themselves and to demonstrate their knowledge, exploration, and mastery of class materials.

It's true that technology plays a key part in the successful execution of video production, but the general availability of contemporary information and communication technologies (for example, mobile phones that record video) renders most of today's students competent, if not proficient, in their ability to use them. Where students lack critical direction is in the potential for their knowledge of these skillsets. All dressed up, and no place to go. Luckily, that's where teachers come in.

There is an opportunity to use video in almost any subject to help students grasp core concepts. Critical to the outcome of using video in the classroom, however, is the simple fact that video is used as part of a lesson as opposed to being the lesson in and of itself.

In the following chapters, we explore this idea before offering some strategic situations in which educators have found success with video production in the K-12 classroom. We also begin to address video production as a craft, considering whether there is a right way to do it as well as the merit in allowing students to use video production as a tool for guided, topic-based exploration.

FIVE

Expression

It was a very cold, January day when we visited Brad Bartholomew, who teaches the video, radio, and communication courses at Lake High School—a small and somewhat affluent high school in central New York. This town of just over 2,000 rests comfortably outside the suburbs of mid-sized city and boasts an impressive statistic of successfully enrolling 90 percent of its graduates in college.

We were escorted to the class by a woman who monitored the visitor sign-in process. This was because she wasn't sure we could find his room, which was off the beaten trail, and, as it turned out, this was a symbol of how the school district thought of video and its place in education.

My first impression of the lab/room, Brad's space, was that it was dominated by computers. It was neat, organized, and well maintained by its keeper. Brad had been working at this school for eight years. He started out in technology and worked his way to video, radio, and communication. He had no formal training in these subjects and admitted he'd learned everything about these areas from his students and by just doing it.

Brad talked to us while his students entered the class, and they seemed to know what they needed to do with minimal instruction on his part. He explained that the students were in the production stage of their music video assignment, working from scripted storyboards. As he talked they were collecting their film passes from a hook on the wall behind his desk, which granted them official permission to shoot their footage in areas of the school outside of the classroom.

This was a special arrangement Brad had made over the years to deal with the special needs of production that often required out-of-class destinations. He told the story of his colleague who taught English near his classroom and was upset with the "open access" policy of his class because it allowed students to, essentially, freely roam the halls and school property while classes were going on.

In her mind, such a freedom was not appropriate for students, and she was not happy that he encouraged this policy. This was before she was temporarily re-assigned to a nearby school—East High School. The video teacher at EHS had an even more liberal access policy that often involved the teacher driving his students, if necessary, to locations miles off the campus to get images they required. In addition to this, there was no real policy in terms of hall passes for students left behind in the classroom.

By comparison, EHS was without limits! Later returning to Lake High School, she acknowledged her respect for Brad's comparatively structured policy of "film passes," which students wore around their necks while producing their videos.

We walked around the school with Brad as he checked on his students. He explained that part of the film pass arrangement was that hall monitors kept an eye on the students as well. We visited all five production groups in their various stations across the school grounds, and they consistently struck us as being serious in their music video production pursuits, as well as respectful of the rules. One example of this was the "no violence" rule.

One of the groups was shooting a protagonist being hit by a basketball thrown by another student—VERY hard. But he wore a thick pad to deflect the blow of the ball as it hit him in the chest. Before they recorded the shot they asked Brad if this was acceptable. Brad supervised the event and it was a smooth, successful, and fun experience.

We talked about Brad's curriculum, the differences between classes he taught from radio to TV to general communications, and the way that he taught them. Our overall impression of visual communication in the curriculum was that media production was clearly seen as a vocation—this as opposed to a means of expression or "text," like writing.

As it turns out this had a particular bearing on the way that the superintendent of the school district labeled Brad and his classes. He basically told Brad, "You and what you do are essentially invisible to me."

Brad felt that this was truly a problem, not only with the superintendent, but also throughout the rest of the school. Such an attitude coming from the top was truly a disservice to the kids, as it limited the potential and reach of video upon the school population.

The superintendent was concerned more with the "core five" subjects in the district: English, social studies, science, math, and foreign language. He did not see any connection between the activities of the communication courses and those five subjects. No wonder Brad was invisible since his classroom and what he taught were both off the beaten trail!

This is an example of how some schools tend to marginalize video as separate from the core curriculum. What Brad's superintendent failed to see was that video (and other media tools as well) can exercise and express a student's understanding and involvement in any "core five" subject, not just the vocational practices of professional TV or radio or communication.

Video as an Instrument

It's helpful to think of video as a tool of learning—among many—to employ in a holistic manner. If Brad's classroom was a "writing room" (rather than a "video room"), the superintendent might have "seen" him and his class because writing is an activity associated, at some level, with every core subject. Writing is widely understood to be complementary to educational objectives across the board, not just the vocation of writing. This despite the fact that some students might grow up to be professional writers—not to mention that it is likely that they will be better writers because of their multi-dimensional practice of writing in all subjects.

Videomaking can be approached in the same way. As a video instructor, I can teach video basics to my students pretty quickly and effectively in the vacuum of a "how-to" activity. But unless they apply this practice to the visual expression of an idea, it will fade quickly. They will learn much more and do better work if they connect the practice to subjects and ideas outside of simple operational procedures.

It turns out Brad had confirmed this when he partnered with a Spanish teacher and produced a series of Spanish language radio commercials. The joint exercise invigorated the respective lesson plans of the Spanish and video students. Though Brad had wanted to do more of this kind of cross-disciplinary work, it was an uphill battle for him and the subject of videomaking to be seen as relevant to the teachers of other core subjects. These teachers seemed more focused on state tests than out-of-the-box teaching methods.

If teachers of core subjects allow it in their classrooms, video can serve EDU-cation just as well as, if not better than, VO-cation. As the value of the practice of writing is only part wordsmithery, the value of video is only part visual craft. The most important part of both is having something to say once the pen hits the paper or the camera switches "on."

SIX

Purpose

If there has been one consistent factor around the success of video production in K-12 settings it has been adherence to the horse-before-cart principle.

The idea behind it is that video production needs a purpose to be successful—especially in educational settings. When there is no purpose (horse) there is, as a rule, no value (cart). The sheer novelty and recreational qualities of the video production experience are not enough to carry the experience.

This is why we work to encourage teachers to allow video production in their classrooms regardless of how little or how much experience they may have with the technology and conventions. The purpose the technological activity of videomaking is connected to matters more than the technological activity itself. And in the classroom, that purpose is a lesson plan. Teachers should think of the process of video production as a blank canvas to paint learning upon.

This said, it is still important to acknowledge the recreational (that is: fun) qualities of the experience of videomaking as part of the reason for success, much like a cart in a horse-cart arrangement brings goods to a destination. It's just that there must be a clear leader in the venture. That leader is an educator with a defined educational objective.

Shortcomings we have witnessed in K-12 videomaking have had one circumstance in common: they were without purpose. Examples include videomaking pursued only for videomaking's sake. Also when the activity was centered on copying something, like a movie, for the sake of demonstrating to others that they could make something that *looked like* a movie, but it was just a copy with no purpose of its own.

This is not to say that every successful videomaking experience must be chained to deeply rational purposes and strict educational objectives.

But if such experiences stray too far from the context of the learning environment, they tend to become purely recreational, self-serving, and, in the end, not all that valuable — even to the children.

Some recent videomaking experiences in a middle school environment provide a good example of the horse and cart metaphor.

Egg Drop: Following a Teacher's Objective

One fifth grade teacher with no videomaking experience decided to use the camera we provided him to record a classroom science experiment. In small teams, students were tasked to devise a means of insulating a conventional raw egg from impact as it was dropped from a second-story window of the school. The object was to prevent the egg from breaking.

After the groups finished, the teacher and a small group of students descended to the playground beneath the second floor window to watch and record the egg drops. Though the resulting video will never win any awards for excellent cinematography (but if there were such a thing as a "seasickness factor" they might be nominated for that) the video clearly captured the educational joy in this kinetic classroom experience. The camera captured each egg's fall and the success of two of the drops. No matter the egg outcome, the students were positively delighted by the activity, and the video camera allowed for future viewing of the event. In the end, the egg drop experience involved a teacher with a learning objective and no videomaking experience: mission accomplished with clearly lasting impact.

Take-Home Video: Following a Technological Objective

In a research exercise we engaged in with middle school students, our objective was to get a sense of the students' innate videomaking abilities and styles. We called the exercise the Take-Home video project, and it involved just that: students taking a video camera home and making a freeform video about whatever they wanted.

We had hoped to capture great levels of student creativity and originality, but what we ended up with was a reasonably garbled, topsy-turvy collection of disjointed randomness. There was little to discern in the final projects because they did not have a specific purpose in and of themselves. We had hoped to isolate their natural videomaking abilities outside of educational constraints, but it was the lack of such constraints — call them pedagogical objectives — that led us to failure in this case.

We did end up adding more clearly defined parameters to the second generation of the Take-Home project, and they delivered success. It was as simple as giving them a clear explanation of what we wanted them to film. This particular experience demonstrated "best practice" tendency when it comes to the role of a teacher in a video activity. The teacher serves as a monitor, interpreter, and consultant in the endeavor, and without them in this role, videomaking success is unlikely.

Interview with a Bully: Following a Learner's Objective

In another research exercise, we asked students to share their perspectives on their day-to-day experiences in schools—to share some sense of what it was like to be a student in their school system.

As they had plenty to say right away, the challenge in this exercise was in getting them to decide which perspective among many to share in their visual story. One group of four fifth grade girls decided that they had the most to say about the bullying problem in their school, so they came up with a list of their fellow students they agreed were bullies and interviewed them. Their plan was to simply ask them, "Why are you a bully?"

This educational objective around the videomaking process was different than the egg drop in that it was coming from the learner in the educational equation rather than the teacher, but it was an educational objective tied to the goal of capturing a student's understanding of something (in this case their educational environment). It would be just as easy to ask them for their perspectives on any other topic from social studies to English to mathematics.

As might be expected, their story plan was not airtight. Their classmates did not take kindly to the notion they were being portrayed as bullies. In the end the "bullies" that the girls interviewed did not say what they wanted them to say, in fact, they often referred to some of the girls in the production team as bullies themselves. Suffice it to say, the exercise taught the girls a lot about bullying that they did not know and, in particular, how subjective the term "bully" was.

As adult assistants to their storytelling activities, we were in the position of talking with the students about their story idea and helping them adjust their strategy to fit the unfolding narrative. The students ended up using their personal lesson learned through the interviewing experience to frame their visual story. They used a voiceover of one of the students to introduce the story, followed by the interviews themselves, and then the concluding idea:

VOICEOVER INTRODUCTION

We wanted to tell a story about bullying, so we went around and took people we thought were bullies. We wanted to know why they were bullies.

VOICEOVER CONCLUSION

So we tried to find out why bullies bullied other people and we got some answers. Mostly they bully because other people bully them and

some of them said I was a bully. But I'm not a bully. But maybe that's
the most important thing we've learned. It's possible for all of us to be a
bully to someone else.

In terms of the horse and cart metaphor, the children's motivation to
express an idea about their educational environment led the video production effort. But the complication they faced when their plan didn't
materialize as they had expected presented an additional critical learning
opportunity. When teachers are in proximity to these opportunities they
have the chance to deepen the impact of learner-initiated objectives.

What teachers who lack media expertise tend not to realize—much
like most beginning filmmaking students—is that the true challenge of
mediamaking has less to do with technology and more to do with its
purpose-centered substance or content. In other words, the key to successful filmmaking has more to do with a filmmaker having "something
to say" than in the filmmaker possessing technical filmmaking skills.
When it comes to video production and learning, K-12 students have a
built-in "something to say" any time a teacher puts a learning objective in
front of them. Making the connection between the tools and the objective
is a teaching skill much more than it is a technology skill: teacher before
video.

SEVEN

Solution

As we listened to the principal describe the challenges she and her K-8 school faced in the coming school year, we were disheartened—and at the same time energized.

We were disheartened because of the problems we were hearing about. Not only were the cards stacked against her and her new assignment at C. William Bingham School, but they had also been stacked against her at her last principal assignment in the district, O'Neill Middle School. The district had proclaimed O'Neill a "failing school" and closed it down last year. Karen Everett had touched failure and was changed forever by it.

She knew firsthand what happened when parents with seemingly good intentions determined the distribution of children in a school district. In the simplest of terms, privileged kids who had someone to look out for their best interests usually wound up together in the "good" schools. Underprivileged kids wound up together in the "bad" schools. Her new assignment at Bingham reeked of déjà-vu.

Ironically though, the more Karen talked about the problems surrounding her administrative inheritance, the more energized we got. The school that our research team would be spending the next year with faced many more challenges than we had realized. This meant that our Smart Kids research project was definitely in the right place!

The Project

Smart Kids is a research project in search of a way to move beyond deficit-centered educational reform. In spite of significant research, money, policy initiatives, and interventions that have addressed educational failure in urban schools, failure endures, shaping the lives of urban youth—particularly poor, Black, Latino, and immigrant students—for the worse. Starting from the presumptions that urban children and adolescents have knowledge and competence about the nature and quality of urban education and that students must be collaborators in urban school reform, the Smart Kids research project involves working with urban students to help them tell "visual stories" about what it means to be smart in an urban city school.

Video and Problems

In our K-12 video experiences over the years, we had witnessed a surprising correlation—call it synergy—between video and problem solving. They seemed made for each other!

Being in a position of observing this striking synergy was a result of working with teachers who had little to no video experience. It was rare when we worked with teachers who had any idea of how they wanted to use video in their classroom. The reason they let video into their class was usually because they had heard that it was very successful in other classes. When it came time to decide how to apply video in their class, the answer evolved into something like, "Why don't we connect video to a problem we're having in the classroom?" as opposed to having video in the class for video's sake, which, as previously reflected upon, doesn't tend to work so well. The problems to which we were able to apply video came in many shapes and sizes.

External Problems.   For third grade teacher Mrs. Redfield, it was bomb threats. There had been a wave of school shootings across the nation in the previous school year and if that wasn't enough, "local terrorists" were doing their best to exploit the fear in the air by phoning in daily bomb threats to the school district. The bomb threats were becoming so routine that teachers and students were scheduling evacuations as regularly as math lessons. Mrs. Redfield felt she owed her third graders more than an empty *don't worry, everything will be all right* rationalization of the confusion and extraordinary insecurity of the past two months.

Together, Mrs. Redfield and her students created a story about the bomb threats using a metaphor of a monster to represent the bomb threats in a movie they made. This allowed both students and teacher to step back from the "real" issue of bombs and project their feelings and creative energy into a story that could absorb their anxieties and provide a place for them to vent their fears and confusion. In essence, we were using the medium of video to help solve a problem that traditional means could not.

Behavior Problems.   Second grade teacher Mrs. Green was having a problem with her students' behavior getting in the way of learning. It was early spring and her kids were showing signs of losing interest in learning and gaining interest in things going on elsewhere.

She decided to point her movie project in the direction of class behavioral issues. She and her students created a motto: *The first time it's funny; the second time it's boring; the third time you're out of here!* Out of this came the story "Comes a Time," about a school without rules where students could do whatever they wanted. But in the end, because there were no rules, they could not learn. The experience of framing behavior in a media work helped the students see their behavior in a reflexive manner and they were clearly moved by it. In short, Mrs. Green found a significant improvement in their behavior after the "Comes a Time" moviemaking experience.

Research Problems. When it came to Erin Bronson's fourth grade class, the lesson plan surrounding the practice of "research" had proven very challenging over the years. Ms. Bronson thought that if video could help her students get more interested in research and study skills, and see the value and relevance of these practices in their lives, it would be a great accomplishment. In her experiences, the topic of research was something fourth-grade kids were not typically enthusiastic about. Our hope was that incorporating video into the research process would "charge up" this lesson plan for her students.

Ms. Bronson and her kids ended up doing a documentary story about the Erie Canal. Following our experience together, Ms. Bronson reflected back on process of working video into her curriculum:

> I think that it motivates kids a lot. I think that it gets kids to want to do more on this topic. I noticed kids when we said "OK, we're going to study the Erie Canal," they were like, "OK, well whatever. . . ." And then it was, "OK we're going to do this [video] project," and then it was like "Oh! Well, now we have to do this because we want to be part of this project!" So they were a lot more motivated. . . . They had to do their part.

The necessary process of research was therefore swept into the wave of their motivation to make a documentary.

The Poetry Problem. Fifth grade teacher Mrs. Catrell's challenge was making poetry meaningful to her students. She connected a music video project to their poetry unit and was amazed at the way video came through. She related:

> Once they started thinking they were going to write their poem and they were going to videotape their poems, it really just, they just went wild with it . . . they really enjoyed what they were writing a whole lot more.

The Business Law Problem. We were skeptical about how Mr. Mann was going to make a video connection to the subject of high school business law class. His specific curricular challenge was "to demonstrate how civil, criminal, federal, state, and municipal laws interacted with each other and how understanding relationships between them could help communities solve problems."

Their video was about the dangerous precedent of RICO (the Racketeer Influenced and Corruption Organizations Act) in its application to alleged gang activity in their neighborhood; it was watched by more than a hundred attendees at a special university screening. The kids introduced the film, and it was heralded as a great success. In fact, it wouldn't be an exaggeration to say that the video Mann's class made achieved near mythical status in the local community. Part of it had to do with the fact that the video looked at the problems of their community square in the eye and presented them in a public conversation.

"The most amazing thing to me as a teacher," Mann reflected after the experience, "is that most diverse classes like this are taken over by the white honor students. In this class, the leaders were all black, every one. And nearly every one of them was having difficulties in other classes."

The Problem at Hand

As Principal Everett wrapped up her summary of the extraordinary challenges ahead for her and her students, we reflected on why we felt so optimistic and inspired. The curious synergy between videomaking and problems/challenges was certainly part of it. And we wondered why video had worked so well as a solution to so many school problems.

Part of it could have be the novelty of it. Video is still a very new thing in K-12 classrooms overall, but who is to say whether this novelty will last as video becomes more accessible to students of all ages.

Another reason could be related to the self-reflexive eye that video provides in helping to better see and critically examine problems in a way their eyes individually cannot.

But this problem of a school basically designed to fail was pretty big compared to the others. Was video capable of standing up to a problem this deep and this large?

The X-Factor. As we left the meeting with the principal, we were all in agreement that the Smart Kids Visual Stories Project was where it belonged at Bingham. If there was an "x-factor" in the past problems we used videomaking to help solve, it was teachers with a lesson plan. In the case of Bingham, it was Principal Karen Everett. She wasn't just talking about the problems she faced; she was also talking about ideas for solutions to these problems.

She'd already been the object of audible student complaints, the most popular of which was, "This place is like a prison!" Karen smiled knowingly and said, "I can handle that." They need to know that this is a safe place for learning and if that looks and feels like a prison compared to what they had before, so be it. But once they start to realize that that's the way it works around here, and it's all about learning, moving closer to the things they want to do in life and feeling a sense of pride in their school, they aren't going to feel like it's prison anymore.

And like the other problems that video had worked with in the past, this one had the makings of a success story, partly because of video, but more because we were working with a principal who had a vision for success, was a real fighter, and truly wasn't going to give up. This problem was going to meet its match in more ways than one.

EIGHT

Integration

Even though it was a research visit, it felt more like a safari. We were stalking a not-yet-seen species in the realm of K-12 videomaking: the integrator. This was not a typical school visit, as most of our work is connected to media use in public schools, and most often disadvantaged ones at that. We were visiting an elite private school in Manhattan. What relevance could there possibly be for typical public school K-12 students and teachers in exploring a well-to-do school with more resources, less constraints, and little to no mandates from distant government entities?

The hope was that within this environment, certain "best practices" might be gleaned from a largely successful media and technology unit in a school setting. And from what we had heard from the person we were visiting, it was a tremendously successful example of how technology and education can work together. Was it all because of the factors of privilege? Or would there be other factors that could actually be beneficial and easily applied to public settings? Our expedition would provide the answer to that question, and we were optimistic.

We showed up a little early for our 8:45 a.m. appointment, early enough to get a sense of the school from the front entrance. Coffee in hand, we watched from a park bench directly across from the school entrance as parents and school buses dropped kids at this pre K-5 school near Manhattan's Columbus Circle.

Maybe it was the beautiful, late spring morning sunshine with a little extra glimmer and glow, but it seemed an extraordinarily happy and positive place to be. Children had a spring to their steps, and mothers and fathers were smiling. The whole picture of the school was very pristine and warm. Inside the building it seemed that even the folks at the check-in desk were more taken by the beautiful day than any sort of imminent security threat.

Sarah Moore-Fontaine was a little late coming out of her meeting—typical of these meetings, she explained. It seemed only yesterday we were wishing her best of luck ahead from the graduation podium—12 plus years ago!

Sarah was a student at our communications school in the late 1990s. In her senior year she had produced one of the most memorable films bringing together original music—produced in her music recording class—with her thesis project—produced in her advanced production class. She worked tirelessly on this project and it came out great. She demonstrated that she could pull off the seemingly impossible and this reflected well on her potential in the film industry.

It was surprising, therefore, when we realized she had gone in an altogether different direction than we thought she would. Though in retrospect it makes so much sense. After a brief stint in the entertainment production industry, she landed at USC picking up a master's degree in education and like many others who pursue a career in entertainment, found fulfillment in more educational applications of entertainment storytelling practices.

When she left USC she went on to work at a small private school in Los Angeles, and that is where she began her experiences in bringing education and media together as director of technology. Her culminating experience centered around the school's trip to the 2009 Obama inauguration, which she and the group of nine students made into a two disc DVD set documenting their experiences at this historic event.

We met in Sarah's office for about an hour discussing everything from the four schools in her current school system, to their educational philosophy, to pasts, presents and futures of technology usage in educational settings. She introduced us to her boss, Trent McMorrow who was the Director of Technology for the schools.

Trent didn't just talk about what they did there at this school. He talked a lot about their very particular model of technology and education. This was when we had our first sighting of *the Integrator*. It turns out that Sarah herself had been given the title, frankly because Trent was not able to think up any better (or more true) word to describe what the person in this position actually did.

Basically an integrator's job was to work with teachers and help them integrate technology into their classrooms and lesson plans to make their lives easier and their teaching better and their students smarter. They identified their approach to technology very closely with Chris Lehman, principal at SLA, Science Leadership Academy, in Philadelphia who championed the merits of technology integration in education. Lehman[1] compared technology to oxygen: "ubiquitous, necessary & invisible. . . . When was the last time we took students to a pencil lab?"

Trent and his integrator Sarah saw these two figures as great educators who provided inspiring visions of what school in the twenty-first century could be. They saw it as their responsibility to apply these ideas to their particular purchase and application of educational resources. The job of an integrator was to stand by the students and teachers, truly get to know them, earn their trust, and lend a hand in improving the learning process and making the teacher's job easier and lesson plans more fulfilling for the students.

The main tool of the integrator was technology, but there was also another that we discovered when we looked very closely—call it a blend of ingenuity, creativity, and courage. Knowing technology was simply not enough for an integrator. To work consistently and effectively, technology had to be adapted with nuance and delicacy to the very particular nature of the learning activity it was applied to. Trent explained that this made *the integrator* a breed apart from technology expert or trainer. From our media industry perspective, it was a very similar skillset we look to build in storytellers. Teaching filmmakers how to do any part of the process doesn't matter unless it can be connected to a story. The best way to train a film director or editor is to give them a story to direct or edit. The story will inform a very particular use and application of technology.

Sarah and Trent did their integrating with passion and high energy. They were genuinely excited about their work and the frontiers of yet unrealized possibilities, as were their colleagues in their Bronx campus. But as with any educational setting, all was not completely perfect in this heavily endowed private school (35K/year tuition).

They had some of the same problems all school systems face including personnel issues, slow/fast technology adopters, leadership problems . . . yes, they were human. But the operating principles behind their day-to-day work integrating technology into classrooms really seemed to work well! From what I observed, the majority of their success stemmed from their model of integration. The reason for their success was not completely due to privilege.

Apart from the swelling pride we felt for a student of ours and her impressive success at this school, we realized our student-teacher roles had been reversed. *The Integrator* had taught us a lot about the synergy between learning and technology.

Teachers ask us all the time about how they should conceive of, manage, and deploy technology, and the answer is never simple because it depends on the unique nature of the learning environment and resources they have. One fairly universal aspect of educational settings is that they have limits. When it comes to technology in K-12 environments, those responsible must do a lot with comparably little resources. Given this, there is a certain efficiency and cost effectiveness inherent in the idea of *the integrator*. *The integrator* allows for a learning-driven application of technology, where teachers can focus on teaching and technology people can focus on inventive applications of the tools at their disposal as they meet the needs at hand.

There is also a biological basis embedded in the idea of *the integrator*. Neuroscientists studying the ways that the brain learns (CERI, 2007) describe the process of integration as the "neural base of learning."

> The neuroscientific definition of learning links this process to a biological substrate or surface. From this point of view, learning is the result of integrating all information perceived and processed. This integration takes form in structural modifications within the brain. Indeed, microscopic changes occur, enabling processed information to leave a physical "trace" of its passage.
>
> Today, it is useful, even essential, for educators and anyone else concerned with education to gain an understanding of the scientific basis of learning processes.

In the end we had found *the integrator* in the person of our former student. But even though we were leaving this particular integrator at her school, the idea of the integrator was going far beyond exotic settings we had discovered it in. In considering the potential of *the integrator*, the words of Edward R. Murrow, describing the emerging technology of television in 1958, come to mind:

> This instrument can teach, it can illuminate; yes, and it can even inspire. But it can do so only to the extent that humans are determined to use it to those ends. Otherwise it is merely wires and lights in a box. There is a great and perhaps decisive battle to be fought against ignorance, intolerance and indifference. This weapon of television could be useful.

And this weapon of *the integrator* could be useful as well in the challenge to improve education through artful application of technology.

NOTE

1. See   http://www.edsource.org/today/2013/chris-lehmann-tells-san-francisco-crowd-technology-cant-replace-teachers/25629#.UQWzaErjky4   for   some   context around this eloquent idea.

Destination and Journey in Video Production

Life's a journey, not a destination. Although the exact origins of this quote are murky (with attributions to Don Williams, Jr., Aerosmith's Steven Tyler, and Ralph Waldo Emerson among others), that it comes up time and time again in popular culture is a testament to the enduring relevance of the sentiment. The quote reminds us that life isn't about a particular achievement or reaching a particular goal; rather, our lives are defined by the experiences we have along the way.

This philosophy offers some key insight when it comes to introducing video production in the K-12 classroom. Namely, while it is important for video production to be motivated (to have a *destination*), the process by which students produce their videos (in other words, the *journey*) is equally important. The stated outcome of a video project may be the same for all the students in the class (for example, to create a short film), but the process by which different students achieve this goal will be largely influenced by their individual interests, subjective experiences, and varying levels of skill.

It's important to note that these factors are descriptive rather than predictive. In other words, there isn't any specific interest, experience, or skill level that guarantees a successful outcome to this process. While students need to be provided with the appropriate time, resources, and support in order to be successful in their video production endeavors, it's equally important that educators allow them the time, space, and room to pursue a process that is personally meaningful. Furthermore, the pursuit of this process might involve an allowance for certain occurrences that are not traditionally popular in K-12 learning such as productive failure and a loose, fluid learning environment.

Productive failure refers to the idea that student processes that may initially seem to fail according to conventional standards (for instance, accuracy, efficiency, and performance quality) may actually possess some hidden value in terms of future productivity (Manu, 2008; Manu and Kinzer, 2009). Productive failure holds that students who are allowed to fail learn from their mistakes and, thus, are more likely to be successful in similarly structured future endeavors. Of course context is key, and the potential benefits of productive failure are likely to be diminished if failure is associated with the threat of punishment. Instead, if students are not only allowed, but encouraged, to stumble along the way, they stand to gain much more from the exercise than just a passing grade.

Similarly, although a certain degree of structure and rules may be important for classroom-based learning, creativity and innovation tend to flourish in learning environments that emphasize openness, fluidity, and are adaptable towards students' specific interests. An activity as simple as identifying and incorporating students' expertise or special knowledge into a classroom exercise may encourage students to develop a sense of ownership and a personal stake in the outcome. Allowing students to partially dictate the terms of the project creates a learning environment where students feel self-motivated to create, innovate, and learn.

Making allowances such as these may not be something with which educators are immediately comfortable, and that's okay. Discomfort, as we'll discuss later, is a productive part of the process as well. Regardless, introducing video production in the classroom tends to work best when educators explicitly acknowledge process and the essential role it plays on the journey to outcome.

NINE
Reason

When you're teaching kids in a setting where the economic structure and the home structure and the skill level are so varied, some children—their world is very small. And I think anytime you can expand that with outside experiences you're expanding everything about them. You're giving them a new reference point, you're giving them new knowledge, you're giving them more critical thinking . . . new experiences they can relate to and I think it's really increasing their brain power.

—Sally Beechwood, 1st grade teacher, Corrigan Elementary

One of our most interesting findings over the years of making movies with K-12 students has been the frequent, unscripted, and spontaneous occurrence of critical thinking. It's almost as if looking at things through a filmmaker's lens materializes ideas and concepts that are normally invisible to young learners.

A colleague of ours in her mid-30s recounted a parallel experience when she took a drawing class. She did not consider herself an artist and was often confounded at her inability to draw anything well. After the first class she arrived home exuberantly claiming, "I can do it! I can draw!"

When asked how she did it she explained that the instructor had taught her to hold a small pane of glass in front of the subject she wished to draw and then sketch on paper what she saw on the glass. Looking through the glass was helping her see and therefore translate a 3-dimensional object into a 2-dimensional impression—the first major step in the process of drawing. The pane of glass was serving, literally and figuratively, as a critical lens to help her see the difference between her normal state of vision (3-dimensional) and a drawer's state of vision (2-dimensional) to form a larger critical understanding of the variability of vision.

45

The Role of Critical Thinking in K-12 Learning

The role and importance of critical thinking in K-12 classrooms is nebulous on whole. One reason for this is that it is difficult for students to grasp. It often undermines students' assumptions of how the world works and as a rule requires a great deal of time and patience to work effectively. Another reason is that it is difficult for teachers themselves to grasp. The overall problem teachers face is that there is hardly enough time to teach subject matters themselves let alone the comparatively sophisticated process of teaching students how to independently think about those subjects outside of the classroom. The ultimate role of critical thinking is to instill a spirit of independent, ever-growing thought toward life-long learning.

Although it is not a formal part or major emphasis in K-12 curricula, it is regularly mentioned by teachers as a hopeful outcome in the total learning experience of their students. And teachers are more conscious of critical thinking outcomes when they are involved in lesson plans close to their hearts. In cases where teachers are looking for added impact in a lesson plan central their teaching goals, they may find utility in applying some sort of videomaking activity to that specific topic.

Learning to "Fly"

Over the years we have witnessed lens-like transformations of understanding in classrooms by applying videomaking to a range of activities.

In a first grade videomaking activity we demonstrated how media technology could generate the illusion that one of them could fly. This created a "behind the curtain" moment for kids who were accustomed to seeing the final product of media stories as opposed to the behind-the-scenes process. The exercise served to build a healthy skepticism about media stories and how images they consumed regularly were manipulated in the production process.

In a twelfth grade videomaking activity we demonstrated how a camera could not only materialize a seemingly inapproachable abstract law concept into everyday life but also attract the attention of their community. In this instance, students produced a documentary about the questionable application of a federal racketeering law to gang members in their school district and community. Simply interviewing those associated with the case created a stir in their community and demonstrated how they could have impact on their community.

In a middle school videomaking activity we witnessed the serendipity of critical thinking when a student produced a story about his school that demonstrated how natural and easy it can be to generate critical thinking with a camera. Sidell was a sixth grade participant in our Smart Kids Visual Stories Project at the Kalet K-8 School, and he was very excited to tell the story about how bad school lunches were. The title of his story, not surprisingly, was "School Lunch is Nasty." Sidell felt the best way to tell his story was the cinéma vérité (literally "truth cinema" in French) technique.

He would bring a camera behind the cafeteria counter to record the making of a typical lunch at his school, and then return to the other side of the counter to get a sense of what his fellow students thought of their lunch. Though he did manage to collect at least a little convincing evidence of nastiness behind the counter, along with an unexpected appreciation and genuine admiration for the cafeteria staff, it wasn't enough to generate the results he had expected. On top of that, all of the students he interviewed in the cafeteria were really enjoying this particular lunch. The experience of using a camera to tell his story was generating a critical lens on this aspect of school experience he thought he had figured out. The experience of making his film inadvertently taught him how to think about school.

Time Capsule

In perhaps the most memorable instance of critical thinking with videomaking, we discovered a way for students to deal with the grief associated with the sudden and unexpected announcement that their school would be closing.

When it was announced that the Bingham School would officially close at the end of the school year, we were as shocked and devastated as the students. When the students expressed sadness we tried to console them, but we found it difficult to hide our own sadness and we had no explanations to offer as we were not privy to the reason why the school was closing nor what would happen to the students next year.

After a little time had passed, and with a little guidance from visiting scholar David Buckingham[1] who paid a visit to the school shortly after the announcement, we decided to break out the cameras again as a form of grief therapy. The idea was to empower the children by asking them to create a time capsule video of the Bingham School—to be the voice and perspective behind the story of this school to those who might wonder what it was like when it was a functioning school.

Along with the passage of time, the time capsule activity helped soothe the students and convert what might have been negative energy into positive and hopeful energy in the form of their video time capsule. All ninety-plus students we worked with at the school in grades 4, 5, and 6 took a picture of some part of the school and added a voice-over commentary about what the picture was and why they took it. On top of channeling their frustration and powerlessness into something positive, the final video was very heartfelt and meaningful for all the members of the school community. It was an exercise for both the filmmakers and the audience in taking time to think about their school and what school meant to them on the deepest level.

NOTE

1. Professor of Education at the Institute of Education, London University, and the founder and director of the Centre for the Study of Children, Youth and Media. He was visiting our university and consulting with us on the Smart Kids Visual Stories Project at the time.

TEN

Invention

Over the years of teaching video production to college students, we've found there are two basic ways to teach it. The first is to take them from "square one," everything from how production practices evolved from early twentieth-century filmmaking to present high definition digital video, and plain old teach them how it's done. This approach is like teaching them a new language—letters, words, grammar, sentences, and like language it takes a great deal of practice to get it "right."

The second way is to just let them do it without teaching them the "proper" ways and techniques—to allow them to express themselves, to apply common sense and get their feet wet with the video camera, and to see what they can do. Out of this experience they usually develop an interest in learning the proper ways, but much can be accomplished with their inventive spirit.

The first way of teaching tends to work well with college students as they have professional interests in the subject matter and the time to dedicate to focused study. The second way of teaching works incredibly well in K-12 environments where there is little opportunity to teach the intricacies of the video production process, but more opportunity to sporadically experiment and apply video to educational contexts. I call this technique "inventive video," a term I borrowed from Sally Beechwood's first grade class. It was while I was working with Mrs. Beechwood and her students on their first grade movie that I learned about a very similar technique she called "inventive spelling" (Adams, 1990).

The idea behind inventive spelling (also referred to as "write their way" in many school systems) is to let young learners' desire to write motivate their adherence to proper writing form and procedure rather than vice-versa. Traditional spelling instruction has tended to emphasize form and correctness *over and before* expression. In other words, students

49

are encouraged to write correctly before they are invited to let their thoughts flow in writing.

Mrs. Beechwood agreed with the inventive approach to spelling. To her, the traditional method could discourage young writers from expressing themselves and therefore instill a negative connotation around writing.

What we have found over time is that our videomaking instills a very similar spirit to curricula as inventive spelling. Our version seems to unlock the moviemaker within young learners in a similar way that inventive spelling unlocked the unrefined, expressive "writer within."

Formal versus Inventive Videomaking

In a recent research activity with middle school students from four different schools, we employed two very different styles of video production processes. Because our research team was being pulled in four different directions at the same time, we had to divide ourselves somehow to get to all of the student filmmakers who were working in teams of mostly two to four. Some students worked on their own with occasional help from other students.

To do this, we split our research team into two groups, each covering two schools. One research group had a lot of video expertise, and the other had no video expertise. We had already trained all of the students on all the video production technology so they could operate the equipment without hesitation. The question was: could the students put coherent visual stories together with very limited technological and artistic consultation? Out of necessity, we had designed an experiment that could illustrate the effect, if there was such a thing, of inventive videomaking.

The students who worked in a more structured production environment scripted their visual story ideas, planned them out on storyboards, and worked with the adults on the research team to acquire video and audio materials and assemble their films. There were loads of instructional opportunities in these structured settings and the students benefitted from them. In the end, the projects looked sharp and had good video and audio production values and compelling story content. Even though the ideas and expressions were theirs, the presentation received the benefits of visual expertise from adult consultants working alongside them.

The students who worked in a production environment with limited technological and artistic consultation also scripted their ideas and ran them by the adult research team members for review and any substantive help they could provide. These students leaned on the adult research team members more for logistical support and general mentorship. In the end, the stories were decidedly heartfelt, compelling, and original, bringing light to student perspectives that are often left in the dark. Their expressions, in comparison to the more technically supported groups, were more authentic and honest in their aesthetic roughness.

An example of this was when one of the sixth grade students, Huey, recorded himself on a laptop first talking about his love of a particular reading group and his subsequent demotion to a lower reading group in the recent past. He then proceeded to turn the laptop camera in the opposite direction showing the classroom he had been removed from and a group of students informing him that he was no longer welcome in the room. This production activity would not have been advised as a formal practice given the fact that the cameras (and microphones) the kids had been provided with were far more effective and higher quality for the job. The fact that this student took a laptop with him as his production acquisition device showed inventive spirit and, most importantly, effectively captured his feeling and the story.

When all ten films were screened together, people didn't talk about the differences between the ways the films were made. Instead, they talked about the content of the films and the value of having heard the students' points of view in a way they had never heard students talk before.

Eagle Eye

In another middle school classroom project students were in the midst of an English project when we noticed another instance of students using school-issued laptops as cameras. The project involved the class's assembly of a news magazine program called *Eagle Eye* (named after their school mascot), and students were all working on separate aspects of the show in small teams.

Each of the groups had their own laptop from the class laptop cart and was compiling different stories that would come together in one class video magazine. One of the groups was having a little more fun than some of the others because they were involved in recording a classmate across from them without her knowing about it. As might be expected, it was not out of the ordinary for students to "goof off" in the midst of their project work, but there was something very inventive about them using a built-in laptop camera as a camera to record something other than the user of the computer in a Skype-style manner.

They were using the iMovie interface to record their unknowing friends and then playing the recorded footage back over repeatedly and laughing heartily. iMovie allows users to select a conventional camera or a built-in camera for use with the software either for inputting already recorded footage or for recording footage live. While the classic adult perspective might have been tempted to discourage these side antics, upon closer scrutiny, we witnessed that they were actually reinventing a production recording process in a rather inventive way.

Video their Way

K-12 students did not have to reinvent technological processes to be engaging in inventive video. Like inventive spelling, the idea behind inventive video is aimed at a particular process of more colloquial, non-professional videomaking. This inductive approach opens a clear path for expression through video in a similar way that Mrs. Beechwood opened up writing as a form of expression without limits for her very young writers.

The basic idea is that students know enough to get started with the act of writing before they have attained a complete grasp of the formalities. The thought behind this approach to learning writing is that the formalities will come in time as writing progresses. The same holds true for video, should they require a more formal understanding of production practices in the future. But as they learn the discourse of video it seems conducive to the learning process that they express their video ideas in their video way.

ELEVEN

Resilience

In our travels across the country we have discovered a very consistent and natural phenomenon when it comes to videomaking in K-12 schools: morning announcements are born for video.

In a pre-video era, morning announcements were monotone recitations of the pledge, a moment of silence, and relevant school information for the day, usually read by the principal or other school official over a crackling old PA system.

Over time, the announcements have slowly evolved with technology, from robotic administrative orations to increasingly spirited presentations led by student voices along with, in braver schools, music and even dramatic performances.

But overall, the morning announcements seem to be one of the more universally distinctive attributes of K-12 culture—something to take for granted like a red brick exterior. With the advent of video and other communication technologies, morning announcements have come even further.

Colorado 7th grade social studies teacher Devon Wood had witnessed the transformation of the morning announcement experience over the years and had discovered that students genuinely liked video announcements more than PA announcements. To Devon, this had a lot to do with the extra richness of the information: "They really like seeing anything that has to do with them in particular," he explained. "Pictures, videos of them or someone or something they care about—the more it's about them, the more they watch it."

Given our technological expertise when it comes to video, we are often consulted by educators on the challenge of converting audio-PA based announcements to video announcements, where the question arises: "What is the right way to do morning announcements with video?" Over time, we've observed two distinctive typologies.

Formal Announcements

Don Black's news studio at a progressive Southern California high school, was a captivating example of a formal extreme of the morning announcement experience, the organization and professionalism of this. This extremely well-coached group of 12–18 year old students was operating along the model of a professional journalistic organization. They had news meetings where they discussed past, present, and future stories including the more academic issues that arose on the periphery of their story strategies.

For example, when they talked about an incident involving a middle school student being hit by a car outside the school as he was skateboarding (resulting in a minor injury), the producer of the story asked if it was appropriate to air a revealing account of the accident from a 10 year-old witness. As they were moving closer to a decision *not* to use the interview, because of the child's age, a very involved and interesting discussion ensued about the journalistic appropriateness of certain witness accounts—not unlike the conversations we hear from the halls of college-level journalism classes.

These were seasoned students who had begun their training in middle school and risen up to the ranks of high school producers, directors, reporters, and anchors. They were driven and disciplined. It was remarkable that Don could communicate so much in such a soft tone. He never raised his voice above normal conversation level even though he was addressing the entire newsroom scattered with more than twenty students. They were tuned to his frequency and responded quickly and thoughtfully in the interests of effectively delivering the news to their audience of more than three thousand in the school system.

Don's journalistic background certainly had influenced the approach he employed in their morning announcements.

An Informal Model

Though informal by comparison, Mark Young's morning announcement program on the other side of the country was by no means undisciplined. Everyone had a job to do and these jobs, like those in Don's operation, rotated daily providing Mark's students exposure to all positions in the announcements milieu. Though it was a news-style presentation, it was based less on a journalistic model, and more on what could be described as an "expressive-democratic" model.

The morning announcement process at Mark's Central New York high school began at 7:30 a.m., well before most students arrived at school. This was the time period that the news of the day was collected from various sources from the main office, to individual teachers and also the Internet. On the particular morning we visited, the Internet was down and that was a significant problem for this group since they had not yet collected what they felt was a sufficient amount of announcement material from other sources.

Mark was calm and poised in dealing with the problem and as the countdown to air approached, the Internet showed no signs of recovery so the students collected what they could from existing news sources and made it work.

Whereas Don had designed his California video operation to emulate a seamless, professional news setting, Mark's operation was built on a more holistic model, to relate to a variety of student abilities and interests, inviting them to find comfort with video in their own ways. His students exuded more personal style, irreverence, and overall creativity in their work because they did not conform to one code or approach to video.

Some of them seemed interested in technology. A handful were interested in news. One student showed us her comedy film she had been working on which, even though it didn't fit into the morning announcement realm, was her contribution to the wider communications organization Mark had created. Others were performers and worked very hard on their "act" to impress, and hopefully find fame in, their high school audience. In talking with Mark, we discovered that he had, over the years, sent our university some of its better entertainment production students.

In any event, as we watched them pull together the final show, we felt like we were watching a presentation of information in this school's style, based on the personalities and interests of its students, more than a newscast per se.

Morning Announcements as "Local News"

In considering the concept of morning announcements in the K-12 experiences, it really could be termed "local news" in its purest form: about, by, and for a school community. In considering which side of the formal-informal spectrum might work best for video announcement settings across the country, it is difficult to imagine there is a preferred manner or way to do it. Though morning announcements may be universal in their K-12 school function, every school is unique in terms of its geographical location, administrative, teaching, and student bodies. The manner in which morning announcements are approached and presented therefore depends on the nature and resources of each school. The choice of method depends on what model best represents and serves the school community.

It was truly inspiring to watch these video morning announcements produced by the students and their respective teachers. The fact is that the idea of *local*—which seems to rise up effortlessly out of the morning announcements—continues to confound leaders in the communications industry. Traditional local news sources—newspapers, television, radio—continue to struggle and often fall in the face of meeting unique needs of local communities. And thus far this millennium, the idea of a consistently successful and reliable truly local news and information sources has remained elusive to the touch and control of corporate control.

We often wonder why our journalism colleagues, who prepare the next generation of newsmakers for the industry, spend so much time teaching their students how to make news like the fast fading local news professionals in our medium sized city. In this light it doesn't seem far-fetched to offer college students an exercise from a truly local context that will exercise their ability to face the challenge of delivering local news in the future—say to do the morning announcements for their school.

And as with any form of news, there is a shelf life to this brand of local news. Devon Wood has noticed this in his Colorado school:

> It's funny, there's a shelf life to their interest in any video announce-
> ments. The longer something stays on the announcements, we're talk-
> ing more than three days which seems to be the typical limit—the more
> they will talk over the announcements. But as soon as there is some-
> thing new, they quiet right down and pay attention.

The point here is certainly not that kids have all the answers adults seek. But rather, K-12 environments are fresh and open creation points for new and inventive ways of doing video.

Part Two

Locks

Behind the Camera, in Front of the Lens: Video and Self-Discovery

One of the benefits to using video production in the classroom is that it invites self-discovery. There are other ways to achieve this, true, but none seem as germane to today's students as the creation of digital video projects. The significance of video for today's students cannot be overstated; they are coming of age in a world that is portrayed by an ever-increasing source of channels, including film, television shows, and YouTube videos. Thus, video has become a key de facto space in which students explore, discover, and get to know the world around them. To invite them to become a part of this process is to invite them to contribute in a language in which many of them already possess a certain degree of fluency.

By introducing learning initiatives that include activities in which students already have vested interests, educators stand to instill further curiosity and interest. Video production, thus, is a natural method for students to make explicit connections between what they're learning in school and their developing interests, lived experiences, and evolving social realities outside the classroom. By inviting students to actively engage *the self* in guided pursuits of lesson objectives, school can become a place of simultaneous learning and self-discovery.

Engaging self-discovery through classroom-based video exercises invites students to make connections between lesson objectives and their own lives. Students charged with the task of creating a video are forced to first identify their own relationships with the subject matter. For instance, a student creating a digital video about a story or book assigned for an English class must be actively engaged in interpretation. The act of producing a video about a specific topic requires students to first identify and then to fill in any gaps in their knowledge of the subject in order to produce a final project that is coherent and successful according to the assigned instructions.

While such active engagement is also possible in more traditional types of schoolwork (for example, essays, research papers, etc.), it is more probable in exercises that invite self-expression, creativity, and, thus, activations of the entire self. By encouraging students to take an active role in their learning, and by allowing students to tailor lessons to forms of expression in which they already have personal investments, the motivation to learn may be driven by self-interest rather than the desire to merely receive a good grade.

TWELVE

Boundaries

After two decades of pioneering work in brain research, the education community has started to realize that "understanding the brain" can help to open new pathways to improve educational research, policies and practice.
—Centre for Educational Research and Education (CERI), 2007

It is widely known that Albert Einstein credited music as a driving force behind his development of the theory of relativity, a result of intuition driven by musical perception. If an inference can be drawn from the case study of this well-known brain, it is that the human thought process is multidimensional. In Einstein's case, music was a garden for the cultivation of a creative scientific idea.

In our K-12 experiences, we have found that videomaking seems to have a similarly transcendent effect, not unlike music, on people who are engaged in it, and this can be used to the advantage of learning.

Suspension of Belief

In one kindergarten classroom we discovered a very interesting case of such transcendence in the making of a movie called *Once Upon a Cold-heart* (Schoonmaker, 2007). Following up on our success in the previous year, the teacher, Mrs. Brighton, wanted to make what she called a "video play" to engage her students in the creative process of filmmaking. Like other activities in her class, the video play would be recreationally based and create a warm memory for students that they would associate with the learning environment of school.

One of the students brought in an idea from a story she had read with her mother called *Miss Nelson is Missing.*[1] In the story a teacher has some problems with her students' disruptive behavior and decides to teach them a lesson. She comes to school disguised as a very mean substitute teacher and ultimately makes her students appreciate how good they had it with her. Once they learn their lesson, Miss Nelson returns to the class and they behave exceptionally well. They know the evil substitute could always return if they were to act otherwise.

When it came to adapting the story to their particular classroom it became clear that the children wanted the story to be truly and believably scary to those who watched it. We were impressed with their natural ability to envision and relate to a point of view outside of their own. We didn't realize it at the time, but there was a developmental term for this particular ability on the children's part and it was included in their elementary school curriculum: Piaget's (need source) principle of elimination of egocentrism in the third concrete operational stage of cognitive development. Though Piaget's principles of cognitive development are often talked about in and around classrooms in this district, they are not completely embraced given their resident strengths and weakness in educational effectiveness over time. Regardless, this was a term to describe children's ability to comprehend a perspective outside their own, and a somewhat advanced skill as far as kindergarten students go.

They clearly envisioned an audience watching their film, and they wanted to scare them. This is why they spent more time developing the evil character than anything else. By doing this, they were engaging in a fairly sophisticated cinematic process in their management of a viewer's suspension of disbelief. They knew their audience would have limits in terms of truly being scared of their fictitious evil character. If they did a good job, their audience would suspend a degree of their disbelief—in other words the fact that they were in reality watching a clearly artificial story on a screen, rather than a truly real and in-person event—and let themselves be transported into the fantasy of the scary story.

Little did we know at the time of this creative planning of the film that many of the children were engaged in an inverse process: Rather than suspending their *disbelief*, they were actively suspending their *belief*! In retrospect it makes a great deal of sense that all twenty-five students were not all on the same cognitive level of development. We discovered this when we interviewed Mrs. Brighton a few months after the screening of the film.

For instance, though some of the kindergarteners could talk about and relate to the idea of an audience for their film, others who may have shaken their heads in agreement and excitement may not have truly understood what they were agreeing with. They were just going with the crowd. In addition, when they were developing a really scary character for the audience, likewise they may not have been firmly aware, on an abstract level, of what they were creating. Because when they watched the final product most of the children were truly scared of the character they designed and filmed even though it was completely engineered in full transparency in front of them.

Something very interesting and unexpected happened when the children sat down to watch their completed movie: some of them actually believed it! Mrs. Brighton explained:

> When we sat down to screen it, some of the children actually wondered whether the story was true even though they had witnessed it. "Was that really you?" one asked. I actually believe there were some kids who graduated from kindergarten that year who thought Ms. Coldheart [the "evil character they created"] might be real.

It turns out when we had been engaged in the process of managing the audience's suspension of *disbelief*, a good number of children in the room were engaging in an unexpectedly opposite process of suspending their *belief*. Because what they were doing was truly scary to them, they were managing their fear by temporarily putting it in the background so that they could enjoy the filmmaking activity, in much the same way that audiences would put their disbelief in the background to enjoy the story.

In later conversations with Mrs. Brighton, we delighted in unearthing another Piaget concept that tripped up a considerable number of young filmmakers in the class: the concept of conservation. The basic idea behind conservation (source = Wikipedia, so far) is that children develop (at different rates) an understanding that although an object's appearance might change, for instance when a teacher puts a mask on to pretend to be an evil substitute teacher, that object still stays the same in quantity. There is not a separate, additional person (evil though she may appear) in the classroom. "In more scientific terms, redistributing an object does not affect its mass, number, or volume. For example, a child understands that when you pour a liquid into a different shaped glass, the amount of liquid stays the same."

Einstein's Point

The point to take away from this videomaking case study is not simply that we can interact with concepts at the core of traditional education, however controversial those concepts may be. More simply, we can utilize videomaking as a learning instrument. Video is not a removed, foreign entity, but rather a fertile field for the practice of learning, in much the same way music was fertile field for Einstein's scientific thought process.

Traditional educational concepts like those developed by pioneers like Jean Piaget have served the institution of education very well, but with the insights and many developments in understanding how the human mind actually works, a frontier of opportunity has opened for the future practice of education. A report issued by the international collective

OECD/CERI[2] during their 2008 conference suggested a way to confront this opportunity:

> A new trans-disciplinarity is needed which brings the different communities and perspectives together. This needs it to be a reciprocal relationship, analogous to the relationship between medicine and biology, to sustain the continuous, bi-directional flow of information necessary to support brain-informed, evidence-based educational practice. Researchers and practitioners can work together to identify educationally-relevant research goals and discuss potential implications of research results.

Videomaking can clearly serve in a complementary and illustrative role in this exciting new direction of possibilities.

NOTES

1. Allard, H. (1977). *Miss Nelson Is Missing*. Boston: Houghton Mifflin. Illustrated by James Marshall.
2. The International Conference "Learning in the 21st century: Research, Innovation and Policy. Sponsored by the Organisation for Economic Cooperation and Development (OECD) and Centre for Research and Innovation.

THIRTEEN

Acknowledgment

The 4th, 5th, and 6th graders arrived in the cafeteria with great energy and, for the most part, smiling faces. It was time for these eighty-plus students to watch the movies that they'd spent the better part of the last two months making. By "movies" we don't mean Hollywood-style, feature length narratives. Their movies were grade-by-grade collections of their individual responses to the question, "What's important to you and why?"

This exercise was a first step of a larger research project in search of student perspectives on school and education. Our aim as a small research team was to get to know the students, to help them and their teachers get comfortable with production and editing technology, and to exercise students' expressions of their worlds.

Having already watched their movies, we had the opportunity to pay more attention to their reactions to themselves on the screen than to the movies themselves. We wanted to know what they saw, how they felt, and what it meant to them when they saw themselves on the screen. Having worked for years with K-12 students and cameras, we knew at least a little about what to expect. In past projects, students largely enjoyed seeing themselves on the screen, particularly in fantasy acting roles and in live camera exercises involving the pointing of a camera—wired to a TV for everyone to see—around the classroom. They tended to "ham it up" and vie for attention. Seeing themselves on the screen generally seemed to put them in a perceived place of importance and boost their self-esteem.

But this project was a bit different from most of the others, having more of a confessional nature. It was about them specifically and what they valued in their personal lives. A student would appear on screen, say his or her name, what was important to them and why. It turns out their reactions to what they watched on the screen were, to our surprise, different as well.

We began with the 4th graders. Their first reactions were mostly expressions of happiness and awe at the size of their faces on the large auditorium screen. But as time went on and the novelty of the screening event in their cafeteria subsided, a discernable new routine unfolded: Most, if not all, of the students in the class of any particular child being screened would burst out laughing, then wildly search the semi-dark room for that child.

It wasn't easy because most of the time the child being sought would have immediately covered his or her face in his or her lap. The unfolding routine on each subject's part included a hearty laugh, a turn away from the screen, and almost always a return look back to the screen to watch the rest of their own performance on the screen. Most expressions were ten seconds so there wasn't a whole lot of time to get used to one person before the next one was on the screen being laughed at.

What surprised us wasn't the laughing. It was the turning away that was perplexing. Perhaps embarrassment? Perhaps peer pressure? And it was interesting how short-lived most of the "turn-aways" were before the students returned their attention to the screen and took the performance in, usually with a look that reflected at least some degree of accomplishment.

For three non-comedy movies, we were generating a lot of laughter! But why? Was it because the students were making fun of and trying to hurt each other? The teachers wondered the same thing when we discussed the screening later. They talked about one particular student who was very sensitive and tended to cry a lot, usually in response to imagined insults from her peers. They were glad that she was one of the few students absent that day.

Having paid close attention to the student reactions at the screening, we remembered the student they were referring to and the response of her classmates, and honestly couldn't discern any difference in the nature of the laughter around her in comparison to the others. At the heart of it, the laughter was pretty equal, which led us to believe there might be something beyond simple peer pressure and playground power relations going on here.

Certainly, the best way to discover answers to questions like this is to ask the students themselves, and there is time ahead to do just that. Until then it merits at least a little thinking aloud to consider what value there might be in knowing.

What do they see when they look into the mirror of the screen, and how could knowing this matter? In the study, we were trying to unlock students' expressive voices through video stories, to share their views of school and effective education. What we've found is that students are not used to being asked how they feel about their worlds. They also have very different ways of articulating factual knowledge, opinions, and feelings than the adults who are asking them questions and teaching their classes. We need to learn to listen to their voices and ways, rather than waiting for them to conform to ours. For instance, most adults don't laugh when they are watching each other on screens. That simply wouldn't be an appropriate adult behavior.

Though there might have been a teasing, child-like quality about the laughing indictments of individual students, there also was a form of spontaneous ritual unfolding. Each student was taking his or her place on a virtual throne in front of the audience, and the sheer irony of their momentary importance could have caused the laughter. After all, surprise and irony are two of the most common roots of comedy.

Why did they hide their faces? In his book *Understanding Comics: The Invisible Art*, cartoonist Scott McCloud explains that one of the most effective weapons of good comics is understanding the way we see ourselves as individuals when we are away from a mirror. He explains:

> When two people interact, they usually look directly at one another, seeing their partner's features in vivid detail. Each one also sustains a constant awareness of his or her own face, but this mind-picture is not nearly so vivid; Just a sketchy arrangement . . . a sense of shape . . . a sense of general placement. Something as simple and basic as a cartoon.

The feeling of "Is that what I look like?" might be the reason why the children turn away from their bigger-than-life image on the screen to confront the differences between the image in their minds juxtaposed with the vivid image from a camera. It's a contradiction not unlike the experience of hearing the sound of our voice from a audio recording and asking, "Is that really what I sound like?"

The most fascinating question in all of this for us is, "Why did the children turn back to the screen after the laughter and the burying of their heads?" The easiest explanation is that, despite the laughter from their peers and the incongruities between their screen selves versus their mind selves, there was still something for them worth taking in. They enjoyed—or at the very least were interested in—something that they saw on that screen.

The late social scientist Herbert Blumer would likely call this a form of symbolic interactionism: how people, young and old, negotiate meaning as their lives unfold in front of them. In the case of children looking at themselves on the screen, they could be seen as confronting the contradictions of their images and making adjustments based on these "comic sketches" of themselves.

When video cameras are part of classroom activities, students in that classroom invariably end up on screens. When this happens, something very exciting turns on in them and energizes the classroom. Though we are just beginning to understand the hows and whys of this mirroring phenomenon, its implications on learning are even more of a mystery, and likely a wide open potential for deeper learning. Because in the end, while a traditional learning activity—say a simple math equation—may be capable of turning on a brain, a camera can turn on a whole child.

FOURTEEN

Paths

One of the most rewarding aspects of researching K-12 media-making is not just the amazing people we meet and incredible stories and capabilities of students that we always find, it's in the discovery process itself. We go to a school looking for something—say, an answer to a particular question—and *always* discover so much more.

Such was the case on a visit to South High—a high school of nearly one thousand students in a suburb of a south central Connecticut city of just under half a million people—in search of Jared "Jake" Jacobson, a former TV and film student of mine at the university. Jake was a bit of a mystery to us. He had attended our masters program in the early 2000s and, as expected, launched onward to LA seeking the fortunes of a promising career in the entertainment business. Jake was above average in all categories, an exceedingly high performer with even higher aspirations and an uncommonly mature head on his shoulders. There was no doubt in the minds of faculty members that he would find success, perhaps as a big Hollywood agent, independent screenwriter, or even a mover-and-shaker producer-type. The orientation of his success would be up to him, but he would no doubt find it.

Jake stayed in contact over the years and seemed to be maneuvering as expected around the Hollywood community, but then he dropped out of sight for a couple of years. As it turns out, he had taken a U-turn away from the entertainment industry and was now working in a high school running the communications program.

This was by no means the first time one of our most promising Hollywood-bound graduates ended up in K-12 education instead. Teaching, both general subjects and video, seemed to be a regular alternative for many of our graduates who, for whatever reason, did not choose to stay in the entertainment industry.

Maybe it had something to do with the common foundations of communication and education, both built upon the notion of "giving to others" be it lesson plans or stories. Perhaps that was a stretch, but hearing from Jake compelled us to investigate further. We wanted to know why Jake was where he was and, for more selfish reasons, what inside perspectives he could provide us in our K-12 video research.

The first hours with Jake were spent reveling in the surprisingly impressive equipment and communication infrastructure he had to work with. Unlike many other re-outfitted schools we had visited, this place was clearly built for media. Whoever put it together had a clear understanding of the differences between normal instructional spaces and media instructional spaces, paying attention to everything from soundproofing to the shape of the walls and the layout of the space. Jake had the resources to work with and his students were clearly taking advantage of as well as tremendously benefitting from them.

Jake was absolutely in his element. His students respected and adored him, which was clearly evident with the handwritten sign declaring "The Boss" that they had taped to the window of his office. Like so many other scholastic video classes I have visited, the students referred to their teacher affectionately by the same short derivative of his last name ("Jake") we did—a sign of their comfort level with their teacher.

Visiting Jake in person didn't really provide any more answers than we already had to the mystery surrounding his being there. He was never asked the big question, "Jake, why South High? Why not Hollywood? You could have Hollywood if you wanted it!" He was never asked because the answer was obvious. He was exactly where he belonged, completely in his element and savoring it.

In most ways, his time spent at the university had prepared him for the challenges of this job as much as the challenges of Hollywood. This included knowing how to tell a story, how to channel technology into meaningful content, and how to capture beautiful pictures and sounds. But his education never really covered the part of his job that dealt with teaching. He clearly had that down on his own.

Once the mystery of Jake had been sufficiently addressed, we kicked into "open mind gear," a state of mind we had always found enormously enlightening in other K-12 settings. In effect, we invited South High to teach us something we didn't already know about K-12 videomaking. Not surprisingly, we learned a lot and right away.

Jake was very excited to introduce his boss, South High principal Lorraine McBride. To Jake, Lorraine, was the shining star of this institution, certainly not the excessively positive manner we were accustomed to when it came to teachers talking about their principals. She, along with the students, was a major reason why he looked forward to coming to work every day. And she was the reason why the media program worked so well at South High. It worked because McBride saw media and the students' involvement in it as fundamentally healthy for and relevant to their education.

This view of media by a school administrator was uncommon in our K-12 observations and experiences. Most K-12 administrators we had interacted with over the years tended to think of media as a basement vocation or one of those programs that looked good on the school's stat sheet but in practice only involved students with special interest in the media. In terms of school priorities, it was seen as tertiary at best.

McBride had a very different view of the role of media in her school, especially as it related to nontraditional learning. Perhaps it came from her interest and involvement in media in her particular education and career and the colorful path she took to become a school principal:

> I worked my way up through making a film in school to get into an art program, and then into history, and connecting those two, and then going into environmental science and connecting that, and then environmental psychology and how it all impacts your life.

> And then, now feeling really obligated to give to these nontraditional learners because some of us took years to get to a place where we could put the world together and these kids can't do that in a traditional classroom.

But Principal McBride's framing of media was not just in its nontraditional novelty. Media production had a much more central role in her view of the school's academic mission. This grew out of a broad concern for the overall health and well-being of students. She found a certain short-sightedness built in to the traditional educational system:

> One of the things school leaders don't really recognize as being valid is dealing with the health—the mental health, and the physical health and the social health—of kids within schools. They [traditionally trained teachers and administrators] don't get that, because they've never been trained to get that. They just look at the academic piece.

> And I'm thinking that's really the missing link towards the academics for many of us who didn't have the traditional paths to getting somewhere. All this other stuff got in the way of our doing well, and if somebody could have dealt with that or validated the creative pieces, sort of the alternate thinking, that would have only strengthened, at least giving us a balance of, "Hey, if we could do that some of the time, then alright . . . we'll do the math if we have to."
> But if you can't do it at all, it's going to play itself out in either complete failure, anger or doing crazy things, and it could have been addressed in school. So it's looking at our responsibility as teachers.

Lorraine created a fitness center, outfitting an old room with new floors, mirrors, spin bikes, treadmills, weights, and even a Wii to promote the

importance of life-long heath. She took extreme pride in exercising alongside her students:

> When I go in there and exercise with them, I'm not "the principal"
> anymore, I'm the person who also wants to be healthy.

She saw media—in particular Jake's array of media classes—as central to
her academic mission of promoting kids' explorations of paths to education that fit them:

> I feel this obligation like you do to help them figure out who they
> are . . . so that they can do something. You know you raise a kid's self-
> esteem and they discover "I'm good at this, maybe I can also be good at
> that."

This was such a refreshing perspective to experience in a world of education so dominated by robotic conformity and adherence to narrowly defined and clearly questionable institutional standards and assessment
practices. What Principal McBride was demonstrating in her approach to
education was that if we truly value the ideal of leaving no child behind,
we have to recognize that children do not follow a singular path in learning. They have diverse paths that cannot be measured in one way. It is far
more important to open paths to learning than to make sure everyone is
on the same measureable one. Although traditional paths to learning
have purpose and value in education, they are not the only paths.

In his 1963 book *Informal Sociology: A Casual Introduction to Sociological
Thinking* William Bruce Cameron articulates a more grand, but nonetheless parallel idea to McBride's:

> It would be nice if all of the data which sociologists require could be
> enumerated because then we could run them through IBM machines
> and draw charts as the economists do. However, not everything that
> can be counted counts, and not everything that counts can be counted.

When it was time for me to leave South High, I felt like I had just arrived.
I wanted to stay longer. This was a very special place run by a person
with a contagious human touch. Sure, her job was to run the school and
oversee the day-to-day, and often unrewarding, academic and administrative tasks of a large high school, but all that she did was governed by
an uncommon and refreshing vision that came down to opening paths
for students to learn.

As far as finding what we were looking for at South High, we found
Jake and a whole lot more. Jake was doing everything that our most
passionate and successful graduates do in the television, radio, and film
fields: trying to make the world a better place by sharing stories and
perspectives through media—the difference was he was focusing on
spreading the techniques to young storytellers and could see the effects
of his work every day, face to face, as opposed to waiting for ratings or

reviews. Much like his hopes for the students here was teaching at South High, Jake found his path by having the possibility to explore many.

Video and Voice

What does it mean to have a voice? First and foremost, to have a voice means to have the ability to speak, communicate, and articulate. To have a voice means to have the ability to convey information, emotions, and subjective experiences. To have a voice means to have the ability to raise questions, assert dissent, and verbalize criticisms. To have a voice is to have agency and, thus, to be an agent.

Agency is not something that we typically assign to students. The rights of students are institutionally limited based on a concept known as *in loco parentis* (Latin for "in the place of a parent"), a legal doctrine stating that schools can abridge students' personal freedoms in order to safeguard the educational process. But even aside from such legal jargon, the role of *student* in the modern education system is to be on the receiving end of knowledge. In contrast, the role of *educator* is to provide knowledge. Thus, agency is kept from students by the very nature of the traditional relationship between student and teacher, which is one-sided and characterized by a power imbalance that is institutionally sanctioned.

One of the primary functions of school is to socialize students, especially younger ones, and for students to learn to observe the rules of the student-teacher relationship as part of this process. Furthermore, students learn what it means to perform the role of *good student* in the classroom. A good student is one who is respectful, polite, and receptive to an educator's methods and who never questions, doubts, or objects to an educator's authority. Good students exist in contrast to *bad students*, who need constant policing, supervision, and regulation.

Video can be a productive tool in disrupting popular notions about what it means to be a student—good, bad, or otherwise. Video production offers students a chance to discover and articulate a voice, and thus a degree of agency, without entirely subverting the dynamics of the student-teacher model. Video production offers students a meaningful form of self-expression that is apart from other options available to them. Why is this? In part, it is a reflection of students' knowledge that media messages are often more noticeable and relevant than other forms of verbal and written communication.

In moving from the consumer side to the production side of media content, students envision an audience on the viewing end of the content they create. This challenges their own assumptions about what it means to be a student—to be a receiver, not a producer of knowledge—and, therefore, stands a chance to change the way students perceive schools as institutions and attitudes about education overall.

Although audience is a key factor in discovering and claiming a voice, the makeup of the audience matters less than the role reversal that is at the heart of video production in the classroom. Potential audience members may include schoolmates, friends, teachers, parents, grandparents, siblings, other family members, neighbors, and even the student-producers themselves. The act of exhibition is simply an act of sharing. In producing knowledge, creating videos, sharing stories, and taking ownership in their work, students begin to discover their voice and, in doing so, begin to consciously cultivate a sense of agency.

FIFTEEN

Listening

The important thing is not so much that every child should be taught, as that every child should be given the wish to learn.

—John Lubbock, 1889

Just what is school to kids? This was the question we found ourselves asking when we learned that C. Robert Bingham School was going to close at the end of the school year.

Bingham was not only the school we were basing our latest media and urban education research on, it was also the place where our kids went to middle school only a few years ago.

We probably should have seen the writing on the wall given the daily news reports about the troubled city school district and shrinking state budgets. There was always talk this time of year about which of the many schools in the district would be next on the chopping block. But this was, in so many ways, OUR school!

If the school closing hurt a group of fairly removed affiliates like ourselves—whose day jobs were based at a large, well-to-do and comparatively protected private university, what was it doing to the kids who called it their school? We tried to imagine how each of us would have felt as 4th or 5th or 6th graders to find out that our school would no longer exist at the end of the year.

Maybe the novelty of the idea would have been funny for a second, in a child-like "I hate school" way. We all admitted to utterances of such phrase at key points in our upbringing, especially those days right before a big test, but deep down, we didn't really hate it.

Parents could have easily rationalized it away for us as a, "Well, you have to leave elementary school some time, why not now?" kind of explanation. Dealing with change is part of growing up, right?

A family member, 72, lamented his emptiness when he passes his old, closed school. "At least your school is still there!" he lamented to his wife when she recently visited her old, and still functioning, elementary school. A distant, but unforgotten memory of a 7th grade math teacher who unexpectedly died in the middle of the school year rose to the surface. No matter what any student could come up with to make sense of such an event, in the end someone, something died and the emptiness never went away.

Grieving

It happened that our research team began student focus groups the week after the announced school closing, so we were in an ideal position to gather their reactions to the closing. These focus groups (comprised of students from 4th, 5th, and 6th grades, in groups of six to eight students) were created as a way to gather a sense of what urban education meant to students and were aimed at achieving the broader objective of involving students (a notoriously absent voice) in the process of curriculum design and educational reform.

When the talking began, we expected them to be much more disappointed than they were. Their first reactions seemed more expressions of relief than grief.

"Maybe it's a good thing."

"It wasn't that good a school anyway."

"At least it wasn't because we were failing, like some of the other schools. It's just because we were bad."

"Bad?" we asked.

The fan of the discussion had lit the embers, as the subject of the school closing was but another log on the fire of their disillusionment with the idea of school. In short, the idea of their school closing was just about par for their expectations and definitions of what school was to them.

School was a place where it was very easy to get in trouble even if you didn't do anything wrong. School was a place where you could count on people not listening to you or what you had to say about anything. School was a place where all suffered from the bad behaviors of a few. For instance, an entire grade had lost the privilege of a graduation ("moving ahead") ceremony when a few "bad kids" acted up during one of the first weeks of school. School was a place that felt like a prison. Why should they care about whether or not Bingham School fell off the Earth?

Acceptance

As weeks passed, the kids shifted their conversation away from the idea of how they felt about their school closing to the topic of what school they would be re-assigned to in the next school year. They were ready to move past the initial shock about their school closing.

What was school to these kids of C. Robert Bingham K-8 School? Based on the first focus group discussions, their school was a confirmation of the fact that they could expect little in their futures.

Mixed Reactions

In terms of the research project, the focus groups were certainly working as we had hoped. We were asking students to share their perspectives of school, and they did so. They seemed to trust us, and were increasingly comfortable opening up.

In our first meetings they displayed a range of emotions, but most often anger. In the second wave of meetings, they seemed noticeably less emotional and progressively introspective and reflective.

This applied to topics outside of the school closing as well. Whereas in the first wave of discussions they may have been critical of and angry about some aspect of their teacher, they became more understanding and open minded to the day-to-day challenges teachers faced, and they expressed appreciation for the secure environment the teachers were trying to maintain. If there was a theme to the first meetings it would be something like, "Why I hate school." The theme for the next generation of meetings shifted to, "We need rules to get it done."

As the students continued to talk, they slowly came back to the subject of their school closing, this time with an element of sadness.

"Why did they make us come here and get used to it, if they were going to close the school?"

"Now I have to make all new friends at a new school."

A Video Component

The focus groups were arranged not only to capture open and honest perspectives from the 4th, 5th, and 6th graders, but also to move to a story phase where students could use video cameras to express and share their perspectives in more of their own ways.

At about this time in the project, we hosted media and education scholar David Buckingham, director of the Centre for Children, Youth and Media at the University of London. We brought him to the school, introduced him to the teachers, and discussed our strategy to move from focus groups to video story mode. He agreed that it was a good idea to capture their school stories and perspectives on video and audio, and through brainstorming suggested one possible approach to gathering their perspectives: "Why don't you have them make a time capsule for people who might be curious about what Bingham School was all about?

Let the students tell the story, and in the process it may help them express their grief."

When we shared this idea with the teachers and student focus groups, they were very excited. We were somewhat surprised at how anxious the students were to tell the Bingham story and even more surprised at the pride they exhibited in taking on the responsibility of representing a school that was closing its doors for good. Despite their initial displays of indifference, later reactions were demonstrating that these kids really did care about Bingham School—and the idea of school in general—regardless of the fact that aspects of their school experience to date didn't seem to make them feel very cared for.

Thinking back to the first time we broke out the cameras with the students, we reminisced about one of our initial surprises. Despite that fact that these students were going to a school labeled "troubled"—they were predominantly from neighborhoods labeled "troubled" and/or "disadvantaged"—when answering the question, "What's important to you?" the vast majority proclaimed "school!" second only to the mention of "family."

Such positive declarations stand in clear contradiction to the frustrations kids shared in the early focus groups, not to mention their day-to-day classroom behaviors that their teachers regularly described as very bad. There were clear moments in the kids' sentiments where they felt school was someone else's thing, not theirs. Perhaps most importantly there was also a consistent sentiment of hope about school and the pursuit of a lifelong learning, something closer to Lubbock's call to instill a "wish to learn."

Conclusion

As parents and careful observers of classrooms in urban settings, we have seen many well-intentioned soldiers involved in the often paralyzing grind of making education work. Like the kids we interviewed, they cling to a deeply held belief in the lifelong value of education and a will to make it better.

And there are so very many ways to make education better. Unfortunately these many ways cannot help but operate in a series of conflicting vacuums. And there doesn't appear to be an effective "conductor" with a magic baton to bring all of these ways in harmony with one another. Until one is found, it is certain that a continual stream of students, as the objects of education, will continue to fill classrooms in search of the good things in life it promises. It is also certain that no one will think to ask the children what they think of what their school is or what it should be. The institution of education was simply not built to ask children anything. It was built to tell.

Given that no institution is perfect, schools will likely continue to deliver bad news like school closings, and kids will continue to feel the emptiness and struggle toward productive lives. But when school becomes the place where emptiness is the rule rather than the exception, where few seem to listen or care about what it's actually like to be a student in a school system, there is only so much time to recover before it passes indelibly through generations as a negative force in their lives. And the wish to learn, if it still matters, will have to come from somewhere other than school.

As believers in school ourselves, we remain optimistic that schools are still capable of rising up to this challenge especially if they stay close to their students. Involving kids in the process of making education work doesn't have to be an indictment on education. We're betting they're ready and willing if we simply have the will to ask and the courage to listen to them.

SIXTEEN

Hearing

There was a time, not all that long ago really, when we were among the little people. By little people, I'm referring to children in the K-5 grade range—somewhere between an emerging child and an emerging young adult: the picture that comes to mind when you say "kid."

When it comes to school video, these little people are not so easy to figure out. What can we hope to accomplish using the practice of videomaking with these kids? They are works in progress when it comes to basic communication skills like listening, speaking, and writing and they are not quite aware of the idea of process, a concept inherent to video production (for example, in the forms of training, planning, collaboration, etc.).

Our very first K-12 videomaking experiences began at the beginning of school: Kindergarten. And we were not immediately successful. Although we left each experience saying, "There's something there!" we were unable to really understand what that "something" was, and it was frustrating. Our basic approach was to illuminate kids on the magic and processes of video. We were the experts with all the knowledge, and they were the little people with their blank canvas of media understanding. We had so much to impart, but when we set out to actually do it, something didn't feel right. We were missing something. The kids were restless and indifferent even when it came to conversation and instruction related to videomaking. Maybe they were just too little?

A couple of years went by, and we progressed well into the second grade before we began to figure out just what we had been doing wrong. And as it turns out, it was not that they were too little to understand; we, the adults, were the ones who didn't understand.

It Takes One to Know One

A television network came to town and shot a news magazine exposé on the subject of kids and sex, focusing particularly on the damage of their overexposure to sex through media. The network ended up interviewing and observing many of the same children we were working with. On a personal level, we felt threatened. The subject was a volatile one, and we worried that the producers (who we knew nothing about, nor their motives) were in a position of misrepresenting these children. We worried that they would misrepresent and embarrass the kids and their school. In the end, they truly did.

Beyond the embarrassment, it was the way that the producers did it that illuminated to us—like a mirror of our own treatment of the youngest school children—what happens when you don't take the time to listen to the little people. The producers got what they were looking for: a scathing indictment on media's role in exposing kids to sex. But they didn't listen to the kids as they were collecting what they needed. In short, the kids were talking about sex and media, but they were also demonstrating a surprisingly mature and critical awareness of sex beyond its surface.

For instance, while they were participating in the experiments and interviews set up by the show producers, they were simultaneously demonstrating their awareness of moral codes and social nuances around sex in society. They were not just aware of sex. They were discussing it in a responsible and articulate manner. But the producers were oblivious to this because they were operating on the same premise that we were employing in our work with them: When it came to the subject matter (in this case an adult concept of sex), the adults were the all-knowing experts and the kids were a naïve and impressionable blank canvas.

The fact was that kids were far from "blank" on the issue of sex, and they had something to say about it, not just as innocent children, but also as young, thoughtful, and involved citizens. In their one-dimensional busyness, the adults producing the news magazine exposé simply didn't have the time or interest to recognize or appreciate this.

We thought back to our own ways of dealing with little people, not just in the inappropriateness of "shock and awe" lectures on video in kindergarten classrooms, but also as parents.

If you've ever tried to compile stories from old home videos, especially for big events and family milestones like birthdays, anniversaries, and graduations you've likely learned that the most time consuming part of the process is looking through all the video to find the shots to use. There are usually dozens and dozens of tapes, and hours and hours of footage on each tape. Regardless of what footage is ultimately used (or not), the tapes have to be mined through to find the right shots for the person or subject matter of the video.

This process of reviewing footage can become surreal, like going back in time in a time machine. The more you watch and become engaged in the task of finding shots from your lived past, the more you will experience the reliving beautifully preserved moments from the past and feel like you're there: at that first birthday party or that exciting Christmas morning or that hot summer day when the little kids made their own little video moment that you didn't quite have time to see back then.

This is the point at which you are likely to relive these home video moments from a different perspective. You may hear a former version of yourself in the background, behind the video camera, and cringe at the words that come out of your mouth. But you will also likely listen and pay attention to what you filmed—this time not caught up in the busyness and technology of capturing the moment, rather savoring this precious moment and seeing so much more than you did then. You might see the little people asking questions you never heard before, see parts of them and their personalities you never took the time to see at the time, almost as if the older, now bigger people these little people on the screen have become were eerily present in their little people forms all along.

What is clear in the moment of this glorious time machine is that the little people are much more like the "big people" they will become than they are different. Certainly there are obvious physical differences, but at a very basic level these little people foreshadow what the older versions have indeed become in their ultimate personalities, quirks, and mannerisms. We just didn't realize—or even contemplate—it when it was happening. The message in this is that kids are not blank slates. They bring something to the table, even though that "something" may be difficult to see or appreciate at first. The key in working with them is to not forget that.

What does all this have to do with the subject of "Where to begin with early school work (K-5) involving videomaking?" For starters, we can engage with little people—even though they might not always acknowledge our effort in an adult manner—in order to help them:

- See themselves: Children are figuring out who they are at the same time teachers are. Watch what happens when you simply show kids a live picture of themselves in a classroom (ironically, a place where they are accustomed to seeing others rather than themselves). They come alive!
- Express themselves: Children have much to say if we will listen. Some of it may have nothing to do with a lesson plan, but with patience and guidance most of it can.
- Participate interactively in the learning process: Think of video as an ally in learning, a way to exchange between teacher and learner, rather than a one-way pipeline.

- Tap into their visual energy: They have much to say beyond the bounds that we place them in. They are enormously creative if given the chance.
- Level their playing field in the classroom: Children who have been labeled as "special needs" or simply sluggish learners tend to show uncharacteristic strength when given the opportunity to participate in visual activities.

In many ways, videomaking with very young kids is like being an atomic scientist and doing all your work based on things that you cannot physically see, but you believe exist nonetheless. If we choose to believe that the K-5 kids have something to say about who they are and what they are learning in school, and we use a little imagination (and certainly a high dose of patience!), we can accomplish a whole lot more than just gathering precious pictures and sounds. But we must be careful because it is far easier *not* to listen to kids than it is to take the extra effort to hear them.

SEVENTEEN

Perspective

It is the province of knowledge to speak and it is the privilege of wisdom to listen.

—Oliver Wendell Holmes, Sr.

Capturing notions of what children think about the world from the position of adult researchers is no simple task. Yet this was the objective we had committed ourselves to in our Smart Kids Visual Stories Project, and the clock was ticking loudly as the Bingham School's very last school year was winding down.

The fact was that we had collected disappointingly little visual media from the 4th, 5th, and 6th grades we had been working with all year. It wasn't for lack of effort or involvement. We had our weekly meetings with the teachers that were very productive. We had equipment in each of the classes, and they were using it on their own at least a little bit to record field trips and special class activities. We had brought in special guest speakers to speak to the children about making video stories and other media works. We had long finished the scripted "What's Important to Me" video compilations of all students in each of the three grades. And we were having very productive and meaningful interactions with the kids in small focus groups talking about what it was like to be in their school.

Even the teachers were a little worried about how little video product we had to show for our efforts. They clearly had imagined we would be making long form movies or TV shows by now. But trying to include ninety students in any kind of coherent video story project was proving to be a real logistical challenge for the handful of folks we had on our research team.

That's when we came up with our Hail Mary: the Day in the Life Project. The idea was to send a camera home with a child and have them document a day in their life and return the camera the next day for another student. We use the term *Hail Mary* not so much as a sign of our late game desperation but as an indication of our more risky strategy of letting the kids do something with little to no constraints—just "letting it go" and see what happens.

It didn't take long, even though all of us expected it to. In less than a week, we had successfully collected Day in the Life videos from three students. So we sat down as a team to watch them and see what we had. We felt like schoolchildren waiting to see what the students had done. Perhaps in this footage we had tapped into the great secrets they were holding and so unable to express in any other way? The more we hoped and imagined, the more we began to feel this video might provide the key to the secrets of the point of view of kids we had long searched for.

This was when we realized that whatever we had, and however good or bad it was, it was something in precious short supply. We don't really have mechanisms to consistently track kids' points of view. So in a lot of ways, it didn't matter what, in particular, was on the cameras the kids had taken home with them. What mattered was that *it was theirs*—their statements, their expressions, their views.

What We Found

We all had expected much more than we eventually found in the footage. In the tightly scripted "What's Important to Me" video they had done earlier in the year, the kids were clearly working under adult constraints. In this video, there were essentially no constraints—just tell the story of a day in your life on video.

It was literally dizzying to stay with their stories. All three were unstructured and extremely difficult to follow, either wildly photographed with constant moves and zooms and over-modulated audio, or inexplicably drawn out, fly-on-the-wall "hidden cams" capturing the minute-by-minute traffic in a private living room. You might say we got what we asked for, but regardless of the chaos, it was still very helpful. At the very least it helped us figure out that we were looking for something between completely structured and completely unstructured.

The Picture Project

Fourth grade teacher Hanna Patrick came up with a fairly simple media project for her students. She called it the Picture Project, which she derived from the idea that a picture is worth a thousand words. She wanted her students to take pictures of things and attach written explanations from their points of view. It would give the students a sense of the relationship between written ideas and visual ideas and show them how powerful visuals could be. She asked for our help in organizing the project and we happily agreed. She was doing what we had hoped she would do with the equipment—making connections between her curricula and video technology.

Shortly after she came up with the idea, we made the decision to expand it to the 5th and 6th grades and added a twist: a time capsule. The school was still reeling from the announcement that it would be closing permanently at the end of the school year, and all students would be reassigned to other schools in the district. Along with our interest in collecting more footage of student stories we reasoned, why not use the picture project to capture their point of view of the school, in particular what it was to them as students? In addition, as part of their grieving process, they were being asked to document their school from the perspective of people in the future wanting to know what the school was like when it was open. They seemed very excited at the prospect of being the ones to tell the story of their school through pictures.

To give the project more "motion picture flavor" Mrs. Patrick suggested that instead of written explanations accompanying the pictures, we use audio commentary voiced by the students who took the pictures. Each student would get to take at least one picture and comment on it. Having learned in the "take-home experiment" the problems that might arise if we gave the children no limits whatsoever, we decided to offer them a set of categories of pictures they might take:

- The physical building
- Fun at their school
- What kids don't like about their school
- The official view: What the principal wants people to see about their school
- The people of their school
- Problems at their school
- What does teaching look like at their school
- How do kids see their school

Even though we conducted the exercise in manageably small groups of three, four, or five kids at a time, the experience of running around the school to collect pictures with them was organized chaos at best. Taking pictures was the easy part. The hard part was running back and forth to class, upstairs and down—three flights at a time—inside and out—rain or shine. And of course, what would any school activity be without the playful hallway antics you would expect of 9-, 10-, and 11-year-olds. It was exhausting and, at times, endless. As we crossed paths with our respective small groups of children we declared, "How can these teachers work with twenty-eight at a time!?" It was nearly impossible to keep four of them to a task! To capture their point of view meant not only that we would get pictures, but also, hopefully, shades and hues of the students themselves. This alone may be the reason why a child's point of view is such an endangered species.

Once we had gotten through all ninety children, we were so tired that we didn't even look at the pictures. We were also conducting this exercise in the middle of the busiest time of year in our respective colleges, so the day job was always around the bend. The pictures sat on a hard drive for a couple of weeks. We didn't watch them until it was time to add audio commentary. To do this we used the voice-over tool on the free Mac software iMovie. We worked in the same size groups, found a quiet room near their classroom, selected the picture or pictures each of them had taken and recorded their unrehearsed explanations of what the picture was and why they took it. The hope was that the commentary would add something to the picture that would further enhance their point of view.

As we stood back and watched the kids do their work—independently, as they effortlessly became masters of the software and hardware—that feeling came back to us again. It was a feeling of anticipation that we had found something rare, something unique, something very special: their point of view. This focused, audio form was comparatively more coherent. Having a little bit of structure seemed to enhance the clarity of their feelings and ideas.

Furthermore, when we arranged the pictures together into one presentation, including an instrumental music track, the student point of view resonated even more. What really hit us was that we were looking at things we saw all the time when we came to their school. But this presentation was allowing us to see these things through their eyes and voices. It made us more critically aware of the school, and what it meant to be a student there. And it wasn't really all that complicated. It was pristine and compelling.

The experience brought some things to life for us about a child's point of view. First, it reminded us how powerful a point of view is. In filmmaking, we use the concept of point of view to limit the viewer's involvement in a story to a particular character's viewpoint. That means we don't see everything there is in the story world, rather only the things the character sees and feels. Certainly the storyteller (in a God-like way) is capable of allowing a view from any point of view they choose. Experienced storytellers recognize the power inherent in a limited point of view that brings a viewer into the position of the character. From that position, viewers are better able to relate to the character and feel that character's pains, joys, and perspectives, in a similarly singular way that we live our own day-to-day points of view from one limited position as individual human beings.

Second, this gathering of a child's point of view was very difficult. Allowing kids to express themselves takes time, planning, and great patience because it's not a neat and clean process. What kids feel is complex and messy compared to the adult and institutional settings they are educated in. Once again, this may be why a child's point of view is such an elusive entity to adults.

And finally, finding a child's point of view is enormously meaningful, especially in the context of school. Though we're not quite at the point where we can articulate exactly why, the research team, teachers, and especially the students themselves were clearly moved when we sat down in the auditorium to watch their collective slide show about their school.

Some of it, we admit, was what media education scholar David Buckingham would guard against: sentimental. Watching the story of a school, only days away from permanently closing, from the position of kids in that school. It would be impossible not to feel sentimental. But there was more. A first grade teacher we had worked with in another school, in another videomaking context said it best:

> After a whole year of teaching the kids, some of them become so dear to you and there are others . . . [sweetly grimacing] . . . there's just that personality, that every day. . . . And I think that the video . . . it brought them back to six year olds for me. You can see their sweetness. And someone like Willy, who tried your patience by 9:02 you're ready to kill. And you see that big smile and that grin. And he really is a lovable kid, but you kind of lose that sometimes. But they became even more lovable in the video . . . that brought them back to being six year olds.

It's very easy to overlook a child's point of view, even when they are right in front of us every day. Though it is not the only point of view in the process of education, it is probably close to—if not *the*—most important point of view in the equation—it is also very likely the most neglected.

EIGHTEEN

Noise

A focus on identity requires us to pay close attention to the diverse ways in which media and technologies are used in everyday life, and their consequences both for individuals and for social groups. It entails viewing young people as significant social actors in their own right, as "beings," and not simply as "becomings" who should be judged in terms of their projected futures.

—David Buckingham (2008)

In our quest to unearth children's visual stories about their school experiences we found it helpful to regularly remind each other what our objective was and how fragile the process of obtaining it was.

You could say that we were looking for the truest form of a child's voice or an honest, subjective perspective on their school experience, stripped as much as possible from influence of the adults involved in various aspects of their education.

Why Voice?

What is the value of "voice," or a child's innate views on the process of their education? The simplest answer is that urban education is stuck in a state of everyday failure. In spite of significant research, money, policy initiatives, and interventions that have addressed educational failure in urban schools, this failure endures, shaping for the worse the lives of urban youth, particularly poor, Black, Latino, and immigrant students.

As objects of this failure students are ideally positioned witnesses to the problems their schools face. Though not necessarily skilled at school subjects, they do possess multiple skills and insights into the problems urban students, teachers, and principals face.

In fields as diverse as pediatric medicine, advocacy law, and urban education, researchers have shown that collaborating with young people on their futures increases the quality of the service.

For instance, Harvard Medical School professor Dr. Michael Rich (Rich, 2007) gave adolescents video cameras to document their lives with asthma in order to improve their treatment outcomes. Rich explained, "When patients are framed as biomedical problems and not asked to contribute their experiences and strengths to their own healing, they are not engaged as partners in their own health care." This simple, but revolutionary, step transformed both the classic model of the profession and the situation of his patients.

Reconsidered in the landscape of urban schools, these findings suggest that students whose lives and futures are affected by the failures of urban education must be engaged not as educational problems, but as partners in the reform of urban schools. The deficit approach to urban education, which frames students as problems that the educational system must overcome, ignores students as resources in a collaborative effort for educational reform.

Finding the voice of a child is about engaging both sides of the nature-nurture dynamic in education. Though there is no shortage of well-intentioned nurturing in the form of top-down curricular imperatives, there is little doubt that the student's voice—call it "nature" in the nature-nurture continuum—is rarely consulted and, at best, poorly represented in the process of education. The first among many challenges in our Smart Kids Visual Stories Project was to search for a way to capture that voice.

Finding the Voice of a Child with Video

In earlier videomaking research with K-12 kids (Schoonmaker, 2007) we imaged we could find it just by asking children what they thought of things in their lives. That is when we realized the problem of accurately representing a child's perspective without tainting it (consciously or unconsciously) with our adult viewpoints. We ran into this several times when we tried to interview younger (K-5) school children.

Following is a transcript of part of an interview with a second grade girl, Meredith, about TV shows she liked to watch. Her mother, Cheri, facilitated.

Interviewer: Why do you like *Full House*?

Meredith: Just cuz it's good.

Cheri: What's good about it?

Meredith: I don't know.

Cheri: You like all the characters?

Meredith: Yeah.

In effect, Meredith was being asked to translate her internal viewing experiences as a child into an adult characterization. It obviously didn't work. We had a similar problem with Jimmy, a sixth grader. We were looking for his thoughts about the second grade movie his sister had made.

Me: Do you remember the movie now?

Jimmy: Yeah.

Me: Any favorite parts, or did you think it was good or bad?

Jimmy: Pretty weird.

Me: What was weird about it?

Jimmy: Funny weird.

Most of these children were simply not comfortable expressing ideas verbally. They would more often than not answer questions with "I don't know" and laugh, embarrassed about being put in the formal spotlight of an interview, a temporary and unfamiliar position of authority. When asked directly in adult ways, children seemed inclined to tell us what they thought we wanted to hear.

Inviting Plurality, Resisting Romance

In line with well-grounded scholarly suggestions (Buckingham, 1993, 2008) to see students as competent individuals, we should not expect one consistent and universal voice; instead, we should expect many voices, perhaps in conflict and or contradiction to each other, when seeking their voice.

In addition, another potential problem in trying to understand children from an adult perspective is the frequent temptation to over-romanticize them. David Buckingham (1993b) warned:

> In the case of research on youth culture, for example, the attempt to identify oneself with the "other" has occasionally led to a romanticization of forms of "resistance." . . . In the case of younger children, it is often hard for researchers (and their readers) to avoid a Wordsworthian marveling at children's innate wisdom and sophistication, or a vicarious identification with their anarchic—but nevertheless terribly cute—rejection of adult norms. The difficulty many adults experience

in listening to children without patronizing them is a direct conse-
quence of their own power.

The "terribly cute" temptation regularly surfaced in the 4th, 5th, and 6th
grade classrooms we worked in. There was a continual struggle for order
in these classrooms. Therefore, the children often sought refuge from
their seemingly overbearing and authoritarian teachers and the "prison-
like" school.

It was very easy to take the side of what looked like a poor and
defenseless student who temporarily lost their privilege to partake in the
video-making exercise of the day. The reality was that the quest for order
in the classroom was a continual battle and a proven and necessary part
of successful learning, and we had to be very careful not to succumb to
out-of-context cuteness that surfaced in many different forms.

The Context of Voice

Advice like this places a premium on the context of the learning environment around the child's voice. What is clear about the challenge in
finding and displaying a child's perspective or voice is that it is not a
straightforward or simple quest. For example, over time, we learned
much more about children when we stepped into their worlds and did
things with them. They would casually reveal their feelings and thoughts
either in their actions or in natural conversations in the context of some
activity we, or their teacher, had constructed. It was neither the activity
nor our interview with them that taught us the most about them. It was
the between-the-lines unscripted and intangible moments that revealed
the most compelling insights into their views of their world.

This was clear when we were conducting an introductory exercise
designed to begin a dialog with the children about their personal views
and perspectives. The teachers and our research team thought it would
be good idea to ask each student, "What's important to you and why?"
and record it on camera for an introduction of each class and its students.
Our thought was that this was a very open-ended question inviting creative and unique responses from students. In the end, a discernable majority offered virtually the same answer: "My family and school. Because I
love my family very much, they take care of me and I want to make them
proud by doing well in school."

Talk about romantic. Students in the 4th, 5th, and 6th grades of an
underprivileged and under-performing K-8 school agreeing that family
and school were the most important things to them? What better foundation was there for learning than that? It was heartwarming to listen to one
child after the other answer this question.

But what does this response—call it voice—mean? Are they telling us
what they really feel? Or are they telling us what they think we want to

hear? Our reaction based in romanticism was that their response was pure. But our hard-learned lessons from past dealings with children said, "Wait, watch, listen to the context of their remarks and see what else rises to the surface."

It didn't take long. After the children performed their socially desirable responses to the exercise, many of them extended their on-camera activities in their own way with their own questions and their own colorful designs.

One child interviewed another about his performance in school. When she asked the boy how he was doing in school this year he said, "Really good!" She asked how his grades were and the boy replied "I'm an 'A' student!" In talking with his teacher afterward, it became clear that he had misrepresented himself on camera and clearly was not an "A student." Did that mean that he was lying? Or, with a little reflection, that he was indicating to the public a certain perception of himself that he wanted others to gather from him?

The truth is, we don't exactly know, at least so far. But what we do know is that the rising complexity around the voices of these children makes us feel like we're on the right track of this creative and crafty subject we seek—the "noise" that children make in expressing their voice. This noise can be very easily passed over and ultimately ignored, especially in a school culture where students are seen as problems and deficits in the equation of educational reform. The fact is that students are potential resources in the struggle to improve education. Video can help with this if we allow for it, but we need to open our ears to the noise that children make about their education. They can be partners in a successful educational enterprise.

Though the term voice may be a rather daunting term when it comes to the articulated perspective of a child or student, whether we label it something neat and clean (voice) or unrefined (noise), it is more than fair to say it is currently ignored in the learning process. Capturing the voice of a child involves not only listening to what they literally say, but also capturing the noises that they make in between.

NINETEEN

Fringe

Over almost twenty years of making movies with kids in K-12 environments, we have learned that there are some things that are simply off limits. These items come in all shapes and sizes, from all directions, and a lot of them are in middle school.

We have only recently begun to get a clear picture of the elusive middle school media-maker, let alone the middle school student. There are a couple of reasons for this elusiveness. Institutionally speaking, students are more difficult to get at in the elaborate block scheduling that moves them from class to class to class, none of which is a media class. Without the comparatively pristine K-5 traditional single classroom space, it is difficult to find a moviemaking space in the middle school space.

And honestly we've always been more than a little reticent about the idea of engaging with the middle school age group, with all its stigma and stereotypes from the raging adolescent hormones to the awkward physical changes that go with the human transformation from sweet, innocent child to not-so-sweet-and-innocent young men and women. This is simply the way, however misinformed, we have grown to conceptualize the American middle school and students who are sentenced to it. All of this was why it was easy to avoid going to middle school to make movies with children and their teachers there. Up until the current project, what little media-making we did with this age group was safely outside of middle school grounds.

But the Smart Kids Visual Stories Project took us to the heart of middle school. Our research centered on working with kids in difficult and troubled schools to tell visual stories about what school was like for them. What better place to be to accomplish this than middle school?

It didn't take long to learn that making movies with middle school students was, on the whole, not all that different than making movies with kindergarteners in their single classrooms or 12th graders in their specialized video classrooms. The administration allowed us use of spaces reserved for part time instruction (art or music rooms and special instructional spaces in or around libraries and technology/computer labs and Home Ec. kitchens). As we used these places for predominantly planning purposes—shooting most video on-location in story-specific places—any room with a basic table and a couple of chairs was a fine place as far as we were concerned. The instances of hormonally-induced bad behaviors never competed with the myths about them, and, in general, the motif of awkward physical transformation failed to suffocate the sweetness in the kids we worked with. Our middle school was by no means perfect, but clearly it was nowhere nearly as off limits as we had expected it to be.

Story Development Process

After all the technology training and warm-up exercises and getting to know each other in the first phase of the project, it was time to get to the substance of the Smart Kids Visual Stories Project. The fundamental premise behind our project was that students were capable of intelligent, helpful, creative, and inventive ideas when it came to the subject of their schooling. If we had the time to ask them and listen to what they said, it should be clear that they were smart kids when it came to the subject of their own education.

So here we were at the point of no return and simultaneously the point of reckoning as far as the project was concerned. We met with kids in small groups and began asking them: What do people need to know about what it's like to be a student in this school? Even though we explained that there were no right or wrong answers to this question it was somewhat daunting to the kids in much the same manner as the opportunity for college students to make their first independent film in a class. There is more often than not a pause to take in the gravity of the opportunity as there is so much that can be said and done.

Little by little their story ideas trickled out. Some of them were exactly what we had hoped for. Inspired by their absolute adoration of their teacher, two sixth grade boys decided to work together on a story appropriately titled "What a Good Teacher Looks Like." Two other students focused on challenges they faced every day in school: one coming up with a story about racism in her classes titled "A Day in My Life," and the other on the difficulties in always "Being New," having changed schools three times in her first six years of school.

Other stories the middle school students came up with were comparatively far from our expectations. While chewing through a particularly unappetizing tray of food, one student decided his story would be "School Lunch Is Nasty."

An empowered team of four girls decided to use their storytelling powers to shine light on a problem at their school in "Interview with a Bully."

In one of the more "appropriately middle school" topics, four girls at another school decided they would tell a story about the most prevalent phenomenon in middle school life in their story, "Drama." In the development of this story, the girls were having a little difficulty coming up with an acceptable story topic and as the end of our meeting time drew closer, we tried a different technique to stimulate their creative thought process. We talked about the idea of how human minds are filled with movies of all shapes and sizes, clamoring to come out to the public realm to be shared. We started with seventh grader Aidila, simply asking her to describe the first movie in her head about her school life. It didn't have to be a good idea or even a scripted film. We just encouraged her to free it from her mind. Following is what she described:

GRADE 6 MOVIE—SCENE OUTLINE
TITLE: "DRAMA"
INT. CLASSROOM—DAY

- As Ms. V tries to cover the day's lesson plan, a dramatic incident breaks out among the students.
- A boy tells the girl next to him (his girlfriend, according to Face-book) that she is ugly.
- The girl proceeds to inform the boy that she is no longer interested in him.
- The boy asks if that means they are broken up. The girl responds, "No."
- At this point Ms. V notices the drama and intervenes asking the boy why he is calling his own girlfriend ugly.
- The boy proceeds to tell Ms. V to mind her own business.
- Ms. V motions for the boy to leave the class, and he does so without hesitation.
- The drama continues to rear its head throughout the school day clearly frustrating the students in the class who would rather be focusing on school work.

Our technique had worked, however "non-academic" the topic might have been in the grand scheme of pedagogical possibilities. And as we developed the movie and shot and edited it, we not only learned a great deal about drama, and the no man's land of middle school in general, but also that it was a relevant topic when it came to education.

First, we learned that students are frustrated by drama, defined by them as personality and relationship disputes within school that get in the way of learning and often lead to physical fighting in school. Despite the fact that it is prohibited for children of their age, social networking (Facebook) generally fuels and ignites drama in school settings. In selecting this topic to tell a story about, these students were clearly not horsing around or being melodramatic.

They were expressing a desire for help from teachers and administrators both in managing drama and reducing its interference with learning. They also expressed their desire to talk about similar topics, but most adults they know and work with don't consider such ideas worthy of listening to because they are not deemed important enough to take seriously. In the end, the girls appreciated the opportunity to express their feeling about drama through the crafting of their story.

In reflecting back to our beginning (and clearly erroneous) conceptualization of middle school, we realized how inappropriate it was to think of middle school as no man's land. The drama these kids were going through and telling a story about was no different than the drama adults face every day when they go to work, and yes even while engaged in the sacred practice of research. It's just that most of the time, we know through life experience how to separate and manage it in the context of work.

The students telling the story about drama opened up the door to this no man's land, and it felt right and not at all foreign to be there in the fringe with them.

TWENTY
Humanity

The representations of African American and Latino young people advanced by the culture talk of adult experts . . . draw on a long tradition of radicalized images that have historically denied the complex and multidimensional humanity of people in the United States.
— excerpt from *Our Schools Suck* (2009)[1]

On the surface, the challenge to unearth or even recognize such an idea as large as *the multidimensional humanity* might seem daunting, especially when it comes to the institution of education, which is, in many ways, set up to ignore it.

Over the years we've discovered interesting and effective ways to connect video and emerging media to learning in traditional public school settings and curricula, including:

- Video and reading
- Video and writing
- Video and science
- Video and math
- Video and art
- Video and special education
- Video and creativity
- Video and class bonding

In this light it doesn't seem out of the question, thus, to entertain the notion of video as it relates to humanity. And when we reflect on our most recent experiences in K-8 schools, it's clear there may be more than a little hope to capture and articulate the humanity in urban school settings.

Writing on the Wall

> A society publicly committed to treating all children as equal can jus-
> tify confining some children to unfunded, overcrowded, physically di-
> lapidated and substandard schools only if *those* children are viewed
> essentially as different from the kids attending the "good" schools.
>   —excerpt from *Our Schools Suck* (2009)

From day one of our Smart Kids Visual Stories research project, it was
clear that the C. Robert Bingham School was destined for failure. First, it
had an unsightly track record on the district's school evaluation scale;
second, it was a magnet for kids who were not wanted or accepted at
other schools in the district; and third, virtually all students of this school
were bused in from other areas of the city even though the school was
surrounded by a neighborhood. It was a choice of parents in that neighborhood to send their children to other schools in the district, not Bingham.

Interestingly enough, this was not a bad thing for our research project.
Our project was about working with youth to help them create digital
videos representing the experience of urban education and, in particular,
their knowledge and perceptions about school through their own stories.
We believed their perspectives could influence how communities, scholars, and educators envisioned and transformed schools in the future.

We were not in search of a school that was functioning well. It made
much more sense for us to be in a place where we could experience and
position ourselves to understand deeply rooted problems in urban education environments. We got that at Bingham. But as it turns out, we got
something much more as well: Piles of multidimensional humanity.

Finding Humanity

What is multidimensional humanity? Certainly some denotative notion of *the fact or condition of being human*, but in terms of *multidimensional*,
the emphasis shifts to the plurality of being human. In this regard, Bingham was loaded. First of all, white students were the vast minority. Second, the school was ethnically and culturally rich with discernable popu-
lations of Asian, African American, Latino, and international students.

Yes, there was plenty of multidimensional humanity at Bingham.
However, in the grind of the everyday practice of education at Bingham,
it was ignored. This act of ignoring was, to be fair, necessary to a degree
to keep the institution functioning, but beyond that it bordered on uncon-
scious.

Take our research work at the school, for instance. When we were
wrapped up in a task of some sort, we often found ourselves ignoring
instances of humanity. One day we tried to take four sixth grade kids
around the school to take pictures of various parts of the school. Their

multidimensional humanity was often more interested in getting into childish mischief than in carefully composing pictures! In one sense, they were just being 6th graders. In another they were not conforming to our institutional expectations of them. Since we had very little time to spare in getting the project finished—after all, we had college classes to teach back at the university—there was no room to negotiate with their childish humanity. In a way, this was a microcosm of what teachers with state-mandated curricula—not to mention the twenty-five plus students crowded into their classrooms—had to deal with every day. Who has time for multidimensional humanity? The object here is not to place blame or criticize, but rather realize that the system is in many ways set up to ignore multidimensionality of kids' humanity.

It is important to note that in applying the concept of multidimensional humanity to students, we are not talking about bad behavior or even immaturity. Multidimensional humanity surfaced in many colorful, natural, and inventive ways in our experiences at Bingham. The problem with it was that it was taking place in an environment that was not equipped to recognize, accept, or support it, almost like taking a large dog on a walk through a very small and densely stocked glassware boutique.

Our aversion to the multidimensional fabric of humanity, like that of the majority of teachers and administrators we worked with, was further aggravated by our privileged upbringing. Principle investigators of our research team were raised in at least somewhat affluent, white suburban school districts where a homogeneity of humanity was instilled and expected. We were all expected to conform to the model of good student, and that model rested upon particular assumptions: that we had functional support systems at home; that we shared very basic values and views on the world; and that we all had the same chance to benefit from education if we worked hard.

The basic problem with such an upbringing is that none of those assumptions is or was accurate, and, therefore, the model of student that we had constructed through our own educational experience—the very model the Bingham School and its district were built upon—was misinformed and out of touch with students from non-white and non-affluent backgrounds.

Because of this, our tendency in situations where education wasn't working well, not unlike the school administration's, was to look at students as the source of the problem rather than the source of the solution. On a larger scope, work to revitalize urban schools is often based on responding to external evaluation or expectations rather than the voices within the community or the school building itself. Our research project was designed to attend more carefully to those voices—particularly the voices of young and prescient students—and to bring narratives of change to the fore. Yet we were often tempted to ignore them in the pursuit of order.

In the end the process of videomaking was a magnet for multidimensional humanity, with the added benefit of making it clearly visible. The 4th, 5th, and 6th graders' Picture Project proved a great forum for it. Even though every one of the ninety-plus students involved had to do the same thing—take one picture of any aspect of their school that was significant to them—their uniqueness, call it multidimensional humanity, poured out of their rich audio commentary that went along with pictures they took.

It really was designed as a one-dimensional project. But when there was an opportunity, however unintended, for the expression of cultural identity, personal identity, artistic identity, the students seized it.

Many of the expressions of identity were based on the students' perceptions of what we as researchers, teachers, and administrators would find socially desirable. We cued up each student's photo, handed them a microphone, and recorded their answer to the question, "What is this picture and why did you take it?" For example, when a 6th-grade girl Zinaria took a picture of two workers in the Bingham's main office, she recorded:

> I took this picture of Miss Murphy and Miss Trifone, the school secretaries, because I wanted to show you who they are and what they do here in the main office.

As a skilled student, Zinaria completed the project in just the manner in which it was expected to be done. Task given, task completed.

The school district also hosted international students, including refugees, exchange students, and immigrants. These students were often referred to as ESL (English as a second language) kids and, more often than not, they spoke very limited English. Kemba was the only ESL student in Bingham's 6th grade class and completed the project without fanfare despite the fact that he knew very little English. We often did not know which students were ESL, so in terms of the assignment we treated them all the same. Kemba took a picture of the school playground and recorded:

> I took this picture because I love Syracuse playing outside.

Perhaps if we had known that Kemba was not proficient in English we might have taken the time to make suggestions about his phrasing, grammar, and mechanics for the presentation. But something about the natural way it happened and its pure and truthful nature added something beautiful to the picture it would not have had without—call it the multidimensional humanity of a boy placed in an American middle school straight from Africa: task given, task made human.

Some children had difficulty in delivering socially desirable answers to the question. Tyronne, for instance, struggled to match his response to the grammar of the question.

> The picture means to me because Miss Albert is the best *(pause)* teacher
> in the hall for doing what her job is to keep children from not fighting.

If his response was to be solely judged on its institutional, grammatical
correctness, all of the loving human elements would have been lost. Tyronne's response was built on his love of and respect for this hall monitor
he saw every day at his school.

Plurality of Humanity

In line with the problem of school systems tending to promote a
homogeneous, good-for-all institutional code, David Buckingham (1993)
cautioned against the very practice engrained in everyday school life:

> ... a view of young people as a unitary or homogeneous social group,
> with specific psychological characteristics. Most obviously, this in-
> volves paying close attention to gender, "race" and social class al-
> though we need to avoid regarding these simply as "demographic vari-
> ables." On the contrary, we need to consider the diverse ways in which
> young people themselves construct the meanings of those differences,
> and how they are defined and mobilized in different social contexts.

In perhaps the most striking display of multidimensional humanity, sixth
grader Gavyn looked at his picture of himself shooting a basketball into
the hoop in the school gym, calmly took the microphone and, with no
rehearsal, rapped the following in one take:

> The reason I took this picture
> Oh, . . . I like to play
> Basketball
> Basketball.
> You gotta
> Shoot it in the hoop,
> Shoot it in the hoop.
> Make that swish
> Like swish swish cheese.
> Swish cheese,
> Swish! Swish! Swish!

What is important to realize when it comes to the multidimensional humanity, whether we choose to acknowledge it or not, is that it is there in
plentiful supply and in clear view of the videomaking experience.

NOTE

1. By Gaston Alonso, Noel Anderson, Celina Su, and Jeanne, Theoharis. New
York: NYU Press.

Part Three

Unlocking the Moviemaking Mind

Media and Literacy

Video production can help students make gains in such areas as self-esteem, self-efficacy, and critical thinking. Unfortunately, many standardized tests make little attempt to gauge changes in these areas, preferring instead to measure students' knowledge in domain-specific areas like math, reading, and history.

The link between video production, intangibles like self-esteem, and standardized test performance is still under investigation. To focus solely on improving test scores, however, is to misunderstand the full range and potential of video production and other media based projects in the K-12 classroom. We can connect the potential benefits of these types of exercises back to storytelling as an extension of our humanity.

In short, video production exercises improve, refine, and hone storytelling capabilities. People become better storytellers as a result, yes, but they also become more experienced in envisioning, executing, crafting, shaping, and editing ideas. In learning how to tell a good story, students also learn to dissect and contemplate the contents of stories. Stories, thus, become a landscape for critical thinking, self-reflection, and introspection.

In this way, we can conceive of video as a new type of literacy. *Literacy* commonly refers to the ability to read and write. Historically we associate the concept with the invention of the printing press, the Enlightenment, and the Industrial Revolution, all of which were factors in increasing literacy rates among laypeople (that is, non-land owners and non-clergy members).

Increases in literacy rates, however, represented a social change that was about far more than simple expansions of ability; literacy was about the transfer of power from those who had it to those who did not. It is unsurprising, thus, that literacy was met with opposition from groups who occupied the top tier of social hierarchies. The Catholic and Anglican Churches, for instance, both warned of the "evil and demoralizing tendencies" of unsupervised reading (Curtis, 2007, p. 9). And prior to the Civil War and the federal emancipation of Black persons in America, numerous states ratified anti-literacy laws for slaves (Mitchell, 2008).

Of course, it wasn't the mere ability to read and write that dominant social groups opposed; rather, it was what these abilities represented—the spread of ideas, a possible questioning of the status quo, and perhaps even an opposition to the existing social order—that worried them. In this book, we argue that literacy is once again at the center of a seismic cultural shift in the ways in which ideas are born, reproduced, and disseminated. However, unlike the past, in which literacy was conceptually opposed and challenged overall, the current debate has do with institutional demarcations about what counts as literacy and, consequently, what does not.

Thus, for our purposes, traditional definitions of literacy are problematic for several reasons. What does it mean to read? And what does it mean to write? Must reading and writing take written text as their objects? Or can we talk about reading and writing in regard to other kinds of texts—video, for instance?

If we are to expand our understanding of literacy, it is necessary first to abandon the traditional definition of the concept. Not only is it unnecessarily narrow but, moreover, the traditional definition of literacy systematically and disproportionately excludes members from lower socioeconomic classes. Furthermore, the traditional definition can neither address nor keep pace with the cultural changes occurring outside the educational system.

We propose a reinterpretation of literacy—one that is reflective of today's contemporary participatory culture, popular culture, and the proliferation of convergent consumer electronics like smartphones and laptops. Furthermore, we argue that video production as a means of storytelling is critical to our everyday lives. We live in a world in which we are increasingly surrounded by media platforms, all of which are actively engaged in storytelling. Video production exercises can begin to equip students with the necessary skills to make sense of this ever more complex world and, furthermore, to be successful in it. However they can only do so if literacy and literacy standards begin to acknowledge and incorporate media as part of their conceptual foundations.

TWENTY-ONE

Reciprocity

Incorporating any new learning strategy into a classroom setting is usually an investment. And by nature, investment can lead to improvements, but usually involves an upfront cost. In the case of videomaking, the upfront cost is something we refer to as the *encoding deficit*.

From birth we are brought up within view of moving image media—games, televisions, movies, web, Blu-ray, iPods—and just by watching we learn how to decode—or read—these media very well. By the time children arrive in kindergarten, they possess, without any formal visual reading training, a strong aptitude for the reading of visual media. The same cannot be said about their encoding skills, or their ability to effectively communicate to others using visual media, thus producing and giving way to an encoding deficit.

Conventional Reading and Writing

This encoding deficit might even be considered an improvement compared to the double deficit that many, if not most, young children bring into their first classrooms. In terms of print media, children arrive with comparatively low aptitude in both decoding (reading) and encoding (writing) skills. The difference is that K-12 curricula from day one focuses on improving these particular decoding and encoding skills and continues to the very end. As there is no consistent curricular treatment, outside of late stage media literacy instruction, of visual reading and writing skills, they reside in the margins of the K-12 experience.

Compounding this unfortunate reality is the fact that the typical K-12 teacher has no more or less skill in visual media than his or her students. Though they can "converse" in the practice of reading visual media like instructional videos, television, film, and new media, they are usually ill-equipped to oversee any kind of a videomaking activity because they have no idea how to do it. And this example applies to new technology developments outside of videomaking as well.

Technology Elephants

There is an elephant in the room when it comes to considering any great new idea—call it supercool teaching tool "X"—for the classroom: How can teachers be expected to do "X," let alone find the time to get up to speed with yet another promising new learning technique? Not only are there many other priorities for teachers in their day-to-day work, but something like moviemaking is complicated, requires a knowledge of specific technologies, and is not at all intuitive for the average teacher. Teachers can't realistically keep up with or identify with every learning tool. What is a teacher to do?

Unfortunately, there is no simple answer to this question. But there is a companion reality to consider when it comes to the idea of videomaking in the classroom. As difficult as the idea of incorporating videomaking into learning is to adult teachers, it is considerably easier and more intuitive for children. Why is this?

Visual Language

One of the first steps in educating our film and TV students in college is to get them to see motion picture media-making as a language. The reason for this is that video looks too much like real life, and the fact that it does creates a problem for the students when they look at it through a camera viewfinder. This is because what they see in that viewfinder is, in reality, far different than what our eyes see in real life. Students tend to realize this very quickly when they make their first movies and they end up looking so very different from what they imagined on the screen. They know that something is wrong, but they don't immediately understand what it is.

It's usually because they tried to tell a three-dimensional story in a three-dimensional way. The problem is that they are working with a two-dimensional medium. Converting a three-dimensional idea to a two-dimensional medium requires a certain degree of critical awareness—in other words, help in recognizing the difference between these dimensional portrayals—and then a lot of translation. It's a lot like drawing.

Encoding and Decoding

The reason why language is a helpful metaphor in teaching video is that it involves an encoding and decoding process. If you want to communicate an idea to someone else—say, for instance, this encoding/decoding idea—the author of the message has to encode that message using selected language symbols, in this case alphabetical characters of the English language, in hopes that the audience it was designed for is capable of decoding that message. Chances are good if the audience is proficient in the English language.

Videomaking involves a similar encoding/decoding process, but the language is different—very different. Instead of arrangements of letter symbols, picture and sound arrangements are used to communicate its ideas. On top of this, the structures and tactics of these arrangements are often very counterintuitive to the process of print encoding and even common sense.

This is much like the frustrating difference that foreign language students, young and old, face when trying to learn a second language later in life. Students of a second language often express frustrations related to the adage, "You can't teach an old dog new tricks." The reason for this tendency is that time fertilizes the roots of our first-given language structures in everyday life and makes it more difficult to allow a wholly different language structure into our thought process. Take, for instance, the order of adjective and noun in the Romance languages compared to English: hot coffee versus *café caliente*.

As young school children are still in the process of formulating their language understanding, they are comparably more open and tolerant of alternative language structures. The fact that they are already fluent in the reading of visual language, as their everyday lives are saturated with visual media, presents a built-in incentive for kids to explore the writing or encoding practices of visual language. It is very parallel to the notion of how traditional curricula teach sentence structure and grammar to primary school students. The encoding skills of visual language are similar in nature and congruent with other language development features.

Even though children are lacking in writing skills associated with visual expression, the good news is that if they can learn and communicate in the high levels of abstract thought associated with written and spoken English they will likely find learning video symbols and expressions easier in comparison. But as is painfully clear with the case of adults learning new languages, the earlier children are exposed to formative, language-like practices like visual language encoding, the better.

Video: A New "Paper" to Write On?

Another embedded feature of videomaking in classes is the broader opportunity it presents for teachers to get acquainted with video's formal features, not so much as a technology, but more as an instrument of education. For instance, social studies teachers are not necessarily specialists in literature or writing, but more often than not they utilize the discourses of reading and writing as instruments in their lesson plans. In this light, video can be seen as an expanded "intertextual paper" to read and write with (Navas, 2010).

The purpose of this discussion is by no means to intimidate teachers about the different and often difficult language involved in videomaking; rather it is to call attention to the fundamental differences underlying the structures of written and spoken language versus visual language. The down side is that teachers have to learn a new language, which is a tall order. The up side is that because it is new and different, it can bring out new and different dimensions of learning that current learning methods (reading and writing) cannot. As there is no question that videomaking can add considerably to learning environments, the only question remaining is whether it is worth a teacher's investment to learn and apply.

In her book *Engaging the Eye Generation*, Johanna Riddle (2009) shared an enlightening epiphany she experienced when she battled with the notion of whether to accept the challenge of videomaking in her class:

> It didn't take long to realize that every child in the school wanted to get their hands on that digital camera. They saw me clicking around campus, honing basic digital photography skills, and they wanted to try it too. They wanted to experience education, not just read about it or listen to a teacher talk about it. Their hunger for a broader forum of communication and creation encouraged me to overcome my first hurdle in this new world of technology application. That moment of cognizance remains one of the great epiphanies of my teaching career—realizing that my students' need to know superseded my need to know it all. I finally understood that I didn't have to have full mastery in order to empower them. I simply had to be willing to learn alongside them, to trust in my judgment and experience along the shared path of learning. That insight changed so much about the way I had always viewed my role as a teacher. It was a definition that shifted and broadened as I realized that we were all going to move forward—together.

She realized the first step in unlocking the moviemaking mind is to have the courage to let go of the idea of knowing it all and to be open to becoming a student in one's own classroom.

TWENTY-TWO

Empowerment

Teachers are so afraid of that word—empowerment. They're afraid that kids are going to take over.
—Lorraine McBride, Principal South High School, in Connecticut

Our second of three iMovie training sessions was underway, and we brought a visitor with us because he was intrigued with our project. Brad Bartholomew taught video and communications at a nearby suburban high school and found it very interesting that our research project involved teaching 4th, 5th, and 6th graders how to edit. He seemed somewhat skeptical of whether they were old enough and capable of learning such a seemingly complicated thing as video editing. So when he asked if he could observe and lend a helping hand, we welcomed him.

All the students had already shot video of their own and it was time for them to learn how to assemble the footage they had shot with video editing software, iMovie, already included with their classroom computers.

We had run the first training session with the 4th graders the day before and on this day we were doing back-to-back training sessions with the 5th and 6th graders, one hour each. It seemed the more we unveiled our plans to Brad, the more skeptical he was that they would work. Would one hour be enough time? Were the students too young and inexperienced to be able to grasp the concepts?

Brad sat back and watched as Jason, the technology guru of our research team, projected the iMovie program on the screen at the front of the room. Jason was a skilled video editing trainer, but the youngest students he had ever worked with before this project were college freshmen. In fact, everyone on my research team—not to mention ALL the teachers at the public school we were working at—had at some point looked at us strangely, head cocked slightly to one side, and said, "Real-

117

ly?" when we suggested that these kids would have no problem learning video editing, and quickly at that. Based on our experiences in teaching kids editing in the past, the best approach was to lure them in visually. This involved putting the video material in front of them, explaining how the interface worked in a basic way, and inviting them to try it in front of everyone to confirm how easy it really was. If our theory was correct, in no time they would be dancing around the whole program and investigating its capabilities on their own.

The session was going very smoothly when Brad whispered to us that he had an idea of something he could contribute to the project. He could print out instructions of all the steps Jason was going through so that the students could have a roadmap for putting their videos together. This was something his high school's administrators had required him to do in his classes and, since he was very familiar with the procedures, he would be happy to do this for us.

Our first reaction was to thank him and accept his generous offer to help. But as we watched, the kids slowly but surely took the controls away from Jason. In a matter of minutes, they were effortlessly editing their own videos in front of the class. These digital natives clearly operated in a different way than the digital immigrants who were training them.

They didn't need text-based instructions to learn editing. They needed to explore and experiment—trial and error technique. Marc Prensky, who coined the terms *digital native* and *digital immigrant* to illustrate the divide between students and teachers in the digital age, elaborated on the tension inherent in classrooms today:

> [T]he single biggest problem facing education today is that our Digital Immigrant instructors, who speak an outdated language (that of the pre-digital age), are struggling to teach a population that speaks an entirely new language. . . . Digital Natives are used to receiving information really fast. They like to parallel process and multi-task. They prefer their graphics before their text rather than the opposite. They prefer random access (like hypertext). They function best when networked. They thrive on instant gratification and frequent rewards. They prefer games to "serious" work.

The problem with most work labeled "serious" is that it tends to be didactic, sedentary, unmotivating, and, in terms of their everyday lives, irrelevant. This is not to say that students cannot do such serious work in the classroom, but rather there are rising limits in the effectiveness of such dated techniques with the emerging K-12 student. This has forced teachers to rethink their definitions and impressions of what they consider serious work, as such methods by themselves (as currently defined and engrained into the fabric of education) are proving increasingly incapable of producing "serious" results. Prensky elaborates on this dilemma:

Digital Immigrant teachers assume that learners are the same as they have always been, and that the same methods that worked for the teachers when they were students will work for their students now. But that assumption is no longer valid. Today's learners are different. Is it that Digital Natives can't pay attention, or that they choose not to? Often from the Natives point of view their Digital Immigrant instructors make their education not worth paying attention to compared to everything else they experience—and then they blame them for not paying attention!

In the information age, students learn many, many things about their worlds in non-school ways. Will schools embrace or cast aside the learning methods their students deliver, at no cost or obligation, to classrooms of the twenty-first century?

Through our own trial and error over the years of working with digital natives, we had slowly sanded down the rough edges of our immigrant accents. This afforded us a reasonably well-informed hunch that these natives we were teaching video editing to would not need printed instructions to refer to after the training session. Instead they would need time to explore and experiment. When we told Brad this, he was at first surprised, but as he watched the kids masterfully relishing the new frontier of video editing ahead of them, it made sense. He concluded, "If 4th, 5th, and 6th graders can get it this easily, I have some rethinking to do with my high-schoolers."

At the risk of romanticizing the ascent of digital natives, it's important to note that they are in fact learners in need of teachers with timeless lessons. The question is: Will teachers put in the effort to engage with a generation of learners with very different learning styles? And if teachers are willing to do this, they must be prepared to learn as much as they teach. In the end, digital natives are not just born and raised on digital media and technology; they are born and raised on learning from it. They are learning natives as much as they are digital natives.

TWENTY-THREE

Transformation

> A world being transformed by new technologies and media as well as
> new social and economic arrangements creates the need for rapid and
> deep transformation of genres.
>   —Charles Bazerman, Adair Bonini, and Débora Figueiredo[1]

Most K-12 teachers we work with don't think of themselves as movie-makers. At the beginning of a project, their sentiments about moviemaking are typically summed by something like, "I have no idea how to make a movie, let alone where to start."

Even if teachers are interested in making movies (or other media products), they don't usually think of themselves as qualified overseers of such activities in the classroom because they've never been moviemakers. They are used to being movie readers, but never movie makers. In media terms, this presents an interesting contradiction. Because if a learning task involved students writing a story with words and images on a paper, most teachers would not have a problem overseeing the activity — despite the fact that they are no more writers than they are moviemakers! The idea of transferring the writing process from paper to movie screens is frightening to most teachers.

Part of this fear involves technological intimidation. There is equipment involved along with all of its complications: acquiring, accessing, securing, operating, distributing—just to name a few. Any technology that is new to a teacher requires an investment in time and skill building in order to bring it in a classroom. We've talked already about the ready-made skill and confidence digital age learners bring into classrooms that can serve to alleviate at least some of this technological tension. But there is an additional factor that challenges teachers even if they were to overcome their technological intimidation: the genre factor.

The idea of genre in a videomaking context presents an entirely different challenge to teachers compared to technology, more along the lines of a paralysis. This is due to the overwhelming number of choices that creators with a video camera in their hands have, not just in media genre choices like TV or film or podcast, but content genres like nonfiction or fiction, and subcategories within like reality or documentary or fantasy or music video or PSA. The challenge is to decide what single direction to take a moviemaking activity with so very many choices at hand, in other words deciding on a genre.

Genre Trap

Genre is a term that dates back to Aristotle and Plato, defined as something that distinguishes a type of something from another. The genre that this conversation is most broadly based on—movie genre—is a type of media text or discourse. The term *movie* also functions as a genre, indicating a particular subcategory of media product, as opposed to TV show or audio recording, with certain rules of engagement and expectations on the part of those who watch it. In K-12 environments we have noticed quite often that the concept of genre is a trap of sorts that limits inventive outcomes that might occur between learning and media production.

Ironically, we find this most often with teachers who have media experience or any level of confidence with videomaking as a learning tool. These teachers tend to mimic existing professional genre forms and practices. They instruct their students to create media works that resemble movies, TV shows, commercials, music videos, podcasts, web series: All in the shadow of some professional model. Doing this creates a certain vocationally-minded incentive to make a video story look like a professional work. The measure of success therefore becomes to master the technical quality of the visual product, putting students at a tremendous disadvantage. The problem is, given their limited time and resources, this is an unattainable goal, and in the end it has questionable pedagogical merits.

Instructors who base their videomaking activities on genre mastering will often ask what they can do to prepare their students for the next stage: in the case of videomaking, the next stage is a college-level study of media—something the vast majority of K-12 students will not ultimately pursue.

Our answer to this question usually surprises teachers. We tell them to prepare the students for everything they can do in their school first, mostly because there is much for them to accomplish on this front. For starters, they can connect their filmmaking to the world they are in right now: such as all of their classes (not just communications), their day-today school activities, their extracurricular activities, their governance and interaction with teachers and administrators.

They are surprised because they are not conditioned to think of the traditional educational space in a visual way. Visual discourse is seen as an outside school entity from the perspective of educators. We simply do not use visual media in the context of school. Instead, we tend to rely on reading, writing, and speaking—predominantly print media. Therefore the idea of connecting videomaking to that print dominant environment is a bit like swimming upstream. There is a similar discursive resistance in the college world as well. Imagine what would happen if we allowed our PhD students to do their dissertations in video, rather than print, if they chose to. It's not only an otherworldly idea in and of itself, but it also is value-laden. Visual text is not considered the same value in comparison to printed text. It is considered comparatively inferior, not because it is truly inferior, but more because it is unknown and untested in academic environments. In addition, there is not yet an accepted genre of academic work that allows for visually produced text in traditional academic settings.

Thus, the complications surrounding this genre factor present educators yet another challenge to endure when bringing the practice of videomaking into traditional learning environments.

So there is a double setback when it comes to the idea of the genre factor. First teachers are drawn outward to media genres that don't, as a rule, fit their learning environments and comparably limited resources. And second, when they look inward to the school system, there are no established genre zones for the practice of videomaking.

Genre Ecosystem

Anis Bawarchi's framing of genre as an *ecosystem* is particularly fitting for the rising tide of K-12 media production activities, as well as the dynamically evolving twenty-first-century media landscape.

In ecological terms, genre is a changing and interdependent organism that both affects and is affected by its environment, rather than a static entity. The elements around genre can contribute to what it is, even changing it when necessary. In terms of writing—which is at the heart of moviemaking—Bawarchi suggests that writing recreates genres as well as genre recreates writing.

In college classrooms we introduce the idea of genre as a series of soft and malleable boundaries. There are strengths in having boundaries. They build audience expectations and involvement because they know what they are getting, like a particular product in a grocery store. In this sense, sugar is sugar and if the grocery consumer wants sugar, they can expect to find it in the sugar section, or in media terms, genre. There are also weaknesses in boundaries. In the case of the grocery store, not every customer is served by one sugar. New tastes and needs evolve over time, so subcategories and subgenres of sugar appear in the sugar section to meet those needs and expectations.

Expanding from this example, school video is a particular culture of videomaking in need of a subgenre that serves its educational needs and interests. When we make movies with K-12 students, we are quite naturally drawn into a genre creation process. This process is a negotiation between existing content boundaries and forms and new and different forms that challenge existing boundaries.

Being New

When we worked with Leia on her story about what it was like to always be new in school, we were engaged in a lot of genre negotiation. This was certainly the rule, not the exception, when it came to working with kids on their stories about school.

Leia had basically found herself in a new school for every grade of her school experience thus far. Some of the moves resulted from her family moving and some from natural promotion to a higher grade. But at least two of her moves to new schools were due to administrative decisions to close schools and move students to other schools.

We began the project with a thorough discussion of the story with Leia and what she wanted to say in that story. The subject of genre came up later, but in clear service to the delivery of the story. Leia did not have any preference for a genre, she just knew what she wanted to tell a story about.

When we introduce the concept of genre to our college filmmaking students, we do it in a critical manner that demonstrates the social construction and dynamic evolution of motion picture genres. We do this to encourage their inventiveness when it comes to genre. How they identify with a genre should first be in service to the story they are telling, rather than in service to the genre. Toward this end, we made a short presentation to all of the Smart Kids storytellers to demonstrate the variety of genre directions they could take in the telling of their story. This wasn't an exhaustive list of the only things they could do, but rather a collection of different styles to stimulate their creative visual storytelling process. Though most of the examples leaned toward nonfiction styles, there were some that also involved fiction-based styles, especially the music video.

To help figure out what genre would work best for Leia, we asked her to write the story down as it came to her spontaneously. She took about ten minutes to write it down:

Being New

> Being new. It's hard leaving all your friends. Making new friends is
> even harder. If you don't fit in with the right people then forget it.
> Being new means sometimes you don't know all the stuff that hap-
> pened. When I did find a friend she acted as if she knew me all my life.
> She is now my best friend and she made being the "new kid" not so
> difficult as it was.

This helped narrow down the genre directions and allowed us to ask
more pointed questions to zero in on this particular story's genre form.
We asked if she would like to use what she wrote in her visual story, or
base something else on it. She wanted to use these words. We asked if she
wanted to read the words or have a narrator read them about her. She
responded that she wanted to read them, so we recorded her reading of
the words on video.

After she got used to the awkwardness of her hearing her voice, we
asked her if any images or music came to mind that might accompany the
words. She was very excited about a song called "Fix You" by the group
Coldplay that she felt would add a certain sadness to the story she
wanted to tell. This was because being new was mostly lonely and sad to
Leia. She also wanted her friend who she had written about to appear in
her story. This is when we came up with a simple, symbolic, fictional
activity of her walking down a long, lonely hall and eventually finding
her friend at the end of it.

Through the combined product all the aspects of audio, visual, and
story form that she selected for her story did not conform to one particular genre, in the end it felt natural and fit the story that was being told.
This particular case study represents the hip-hop-like nature of the still
evolving genre of school video (if there is such a thing). Like hip-hop, K-
12 video is one part old and one part new. In the end the blend feels
original and fitting for the content.

In addition to the creative negotiation that was going on, the process
was clearly also a negotiation between student and teacher, with one
constant: the content behind the genre. Genre is a condition around content, not the content itself. Genre should serve the content and the students who create it. If the teacher is the originator of the content of the
videomaking activity, they can shape the genre to fit the content, and
essentially reinvent genres as they fit the lesson plan.

When it comes to K-12 media production, the significance of genre
encourages teachers to take ownership of what once were exotic practices—movies and TV shows made in New York and Hollywood—from
lands far away. Movies once were the purview of others, but now that we
can make them in schools it's time to stake a claim on the genre of moviemaking itself and give it an educational twist.

If teachers can read a movie, why can't they write one too? They may not be the next Spike Lee, but in an ecological sense, they don't have to be. In this ecosystem, where there's a will, there's a movie.

NOTE

1. From their introduction to *Genre in a Changing World* (2009).

The Mess Is the Message

By now it's apparent that incorporating video production in the K-12 classroom isn't always neat and precise. As the previous chapters make clear, introducing video production in the classroom requires a certain willingness to allow students to become an active part of the educational equation.

Video production exercises, thus, can inherently challenge *didactic learning*, which emphasizes clearly demarcated roles and outcomes in the classroom. The didactic method of learning is very common in the American education system. Outcomes are generally focused on cognition and demonstrations of knowledge acquisition in the short term. In the didactic method, teachers are knowledge bearers and students are knowledge receivers. The relationship between teachers and students, as referenced earlier, is one-way.

Video production is more aligned with experiential learning, a learning style that emphasizes the acquisition of knowledge through hands-on experiences and fluid structures. Student and teacher roles are still defined in experiential learning, but the relationship between them is more fluid and informed by a two-way style of communication in which student feedback is a critical part of the learning process.

The complexities of actually doing video production in the K-12 classroom can perhaps best be summarized by the following: The mess is the message. This saying takes its cue from the work of Marshall McLuhan who coined the phrase "the medium is the message" (McLuhan, 1964/1994) to talk about how technologies shape content.

The mess is the message. This finding is an important reminder of the fact that video production in the K-12 classroom is process-based, meaning that the experience of acquiring knowledge is just as important as the demonstration of knowledge. Hopefully, this finding will provide some refuge when encountering confusion, uncertainty, or even a radical departure from the intended lesson when using video production in the classroom. It's easy to have tunnel vision, concentrating solely on outcomes and constantly making efforts to move students toward that goal.

Although the outcome is clearly important as a demonstration of student learning, the process of creation is also significant. During this process it is possible—and even likely—that students and educators may encounter dead-ends, feelings of frustration, and frequent and continuous adjustments to their original ideas. Such instances may seem to suggest that the intervention is failing; on the contrary, they are an expected part of the process and can be a productive part of the learning process.

Video production is extremely adaptable and can be successful in numerous settings and circumstances, but only when it is used organically. Successful endeavors in video production in the K-12 classroom require vision, purpose, and structure, but they also require flexibility, commitment to process, and strategic risk-taking.

Evaluations that are not based solely on outcomes are also necessary when assessing the success of the intervention. To focus solely on outcome is to sacrifice the journey for the sake of the destination. We must suppress the instinct to focus only on outcome, and, at first, it may feel unnatural to do so, especially on account of the fact that education tends to value outcome-based processes and measurements. In spite of the emphasis on outcome, it is essential to remember that destination cannot be reached without first enduring a journey, however uncomfortable, divergent, or messy it may be.

TWENTY-FOUR

Motive

Preparing future movers and shakers for the film and television industries involves introducing them to the often painful negotiation between art and commerce. It's one thing to make a film or have an idea; it's quite another to sell it to an audience at the same time.

This is why we introduce them to both the art of visual storytelling and the profit motive behind that art at the same time. In the end a successful film or TV show has to meet needs beyond the creator, so it can't be just a good idea to the creator. It has to be a good idea to the audience, and it has to attract a large enough audience to pay for the production. Through repetition and practice, students become professionally inclined creators of visual media by successfully walking the line between the creative story they want to tell and the profit motive that pays for it.

The great thing about moviemaking in K-12 schools is that there is no profit motive to worry about. But there is another motive that must be dealt with at some point: the learning motive.

Profit versus Learning

What is the difference between stories made in the contexts of these respective motives? Visual stories created from a profit motive are audience-centered. They seek quantities of viewers: The more viewers that can be attracted to the story and watch it, the better. Being involved in a pursuit of this nature puts storytellers in fierce competition with each other for audience reaction: who can tell the best stories (in terms of critical acclaim); who can tell the most beautiful stories (involving the most sophisticated visual and audio effects); who can tell the most popular stories (highest rated, most watched). The obvious problem with material motive like this behind videomaking in schools is that it puts students in a very unrealistic position: to seek critical acclaim in competition with others who most certainly will have more experience and resources. Thus, much, if not all, of the road to success in such a pursuit will be filled with failure.

Visual stories created from a learning motive are artist or maker-centered. They seek discovery, insight, and knowledge out of the experience of making a movie toward a predetermined, teacher-defined learning objective. The experience is successful if it puts the student filmmaker(s) in a position of taking ownership of a lesson. It doesn't matter how many people watch such a story, in terms of the educational value, or how many awards it wins as long as the experience of making it delivers the lesson plan to the visual creator. The more there is to learn in a subject, the richer the videomaking experience can be.

Over time we have also learned that stories created from a learning motive have a very different aesthetic. Considering that stories made in the realm of profit motive are expected to perform to the highest artistic standards and expectations of visual image forms and genres they can only be deemed successful if they are "beautiful" to their targeted audience.

As long as stories created in the realm of learning are connected to a learning outcome they need only to be beautiful to their creators. Why is this? Because the motive behind their making is more about the active and participatory experience and doing of a lesson plan than the final product.

Keith Devlin (2011) illustrated this in relation to the school subject of mathematics, in particular the use of video games to bring dimension to the practice mathematics:

> [M]athematics is not about acquiring basic skill or learning formulas. It's a way of thinking about problems in the world. The skills are merely the tools you need in order to do that thinking. Math is not a body of knowledge, it's something you *do*. And the printed word can be a terribly inefficient way to learn how to do something. . . . for example, if you want to learn to play chess, you can learn the rules from a book, but you won't learn to play chess until you start playing games. The same is true for learning to ride a bicycle, learning to swim, to ski, to play tennis, or to play the guitar.

Our recent work with a 6th grade class at Frederick K-8 School demonstrated the learning motive in practice. We had worked with Derek at another middle school the year before this project and had the time to make him comfortable with videomaking technology. After a year of working together we left him with a simple camera kit in hopes that he would find a way to use it in his new school. It didn't take long before he came up with an idea in the form of the Eagle Eye project.

For an assignment in his English class, he wanted to focus on the process of editing written works, in other words, the process of re-working a first draft into a more effective final draft after receiving feedback. Editing had always been a lesson he found very challenging to get through to students. But, after he watched a movie being made with iMovie software the year before, he realized he could teach the concept of editing. In short, he realized he could more effectively develop an appreciation and understanding of the editing process, while doing something that fascinated his class: making a movie. If he could get his students to appreciate the process of editing, it didn't matter what medium they used, as much as it mattered that the students experienced the joy of *re-making* something into something better using the editing process.

His idea was to have the class create a news magazine show about issues of their school and have small groups create different stories for the show. Through this video experience he would demonstrate to them how much better their second drafts of video stories were once they had been re-edited and reconsidered in a thoughtful editing process.

Eagle Eye and the Incarnation of Writing

In the end, Derek's Eagle Eye project was a success on both expected and unexpected fronts. First, the project was an example of an increasing move on our part to take a step away from classrooms as video technology and form consultants. Derek and his class were largely independent in this activity and they figured the experience out and made it work on their own. This is very important in advocating the idea of incorporating videomaking in K-12 classrooms, as it should be doable.

It is important to acknowledge that the experience was not without flaws, difficulties, and disappointments. Derek was not happy with the work of a small handful of the more than twenty-five students in his class. These students did not embrace and put themselves into the writing aspect of the experience the way he had hoped. And the school was not quite ready for the impact of a videomaking exercise on the everyday activities of the traditional practice of education. For instance, one group decided they wanted to do a story about school security, so they went to the head of security with a video camera and informed the man that they needed to do an interview with him. The head of security, though a very nice and approachable person by nature, was confused and caught off-guard by not only the impact of a camera being thrust into his face, but also—in the absence of any explanation or context—the inherent role reversal presented in the act of children questioning his authority.

Initial incidents like this led to a pause in videomaking activities. Derek realized the necessity for him and the students to create a process of information, clearance, and scheduling that would avoid putting staff and students of the school on the spot. In this lesson phase of the Eagle

Eye project they learned two things: first, that they needed a process for their videomaking activities. But something else was clear after the principal of the school spoke with Derek after the incident. Even though the status quo had been threatened by the unchecked and unexpected flurry of videomaking activities in the school, the school community was talking about it and they were clearly energized by the experience despite the fact that some changes in approach were necessary.

Most importantly of all, however, the lesson plan was coming to life, certainly in the way that Derek had hoped, and also in additional unexpected ways. In the same way that Keith Devlin talked about the fact that math was not a body of knowledge, but rather something we do, Derek was finding the videomaking experience was bringing the practice of writing to life. The Eagle Eye project was slowly but surely becoming an incarnation of the writing process. Students were not just writing their stories in response to an assignment sheet and handing them in. They were pitching ideas and often re-pitching when Derek told them they could do better. And the students were not reacting to the challenge in an academic assignment way. They were going back to make their Eagle Eye story better for broadcast.

The students who had been sent away from the security officer were forced to rethink their approach to an information source and understand that source in a more complex, human way. They were learning about the responsibility that writers have to not only readers, but also their subjects they write about.

They were learning how to collaborate as writers and how they could connect their own ideas with others to give extra life and resonance to subjects they wrote about. This was particularly evident when it was time to talk about the opening to their news magazine show. In this video piece they would have to agree upon a collective identity and represent it in their own stories. The basic idea behind their opening was that their mascot (the Frederick Eagle) was a strong creature with great vision from above. They used that idea to incorporate in their writing identities— each of their stories would serve as "eagle eye perspectives" on their school. What had always been a solitary experience to them (writing in a vacuum of their own voice as a student in response to an assignment) was becoming a collaborative enterprise that required an entire rethinking of what writing was. The bottom line was that they were *doing* writing.

In the end, visual stories conceived and created out of the motive to learn are by no means any easier (or more difficult) than visual stories created out of the motive to achieve public (and financial) impact. They are just different: suited for the respective environments they are in. But there is an extra advantage for K-12 filmmakers engaged in the pursuit of learning. The learning motive inspires a new, fresh, and truly unique storytelling genre that presents young videomakers with a wide open frontier of possibilities for not only aesthetic achievement, but, more importantly, learning achievement.

TWENTY-FIVE

Confabulation

> Let us record the atoms as they fall upon the mind in the order in which they fall, let us trace the pattern, however disconnected and incoherent in appearance, which each sight or incident scores upon the consciousness. Let us not take it for granted that life exists more fully in what is commonly thought big than in what is commonly thought small. . .
> —Virginia Woolf (1925) on the inherently human dimension of writing

Recent brain research (Gazzaniga, 2012) has shed fresh light on the fascinating way the human mind makes sense of the often overwhelmingly complex (even chaotic) world it exists in. From Woolf's perspective, clearly ahead of her time in 1925, there was a certain atomic level beauty in the complexities that fell upon the mind. Her words were meant to encourage writers to savor these complexities before reducing them to simple explanations or writing forms.

Michael Gazzaniga examined the other side of this equation, particularly how the mind not only searched for clarity in the chaotic, but also how it instinctually preferred such clarity, through a process he termed *confabulation*. This process could be seen in split-brain patients presented with contradictory visual information:

> What was interesting was that the left hemisphere did not say, "I don't know," which was the correct answer. It made up a post hoc answer that fit the situation. It confabulated, taking cues from what it knew and putting them together in an answer that made sense. We called this left-hemisphere process the interpreter. It is the left hemisphere that engages in the human tendency to find order in chaos, that tries to fit everything into a story and put it into a context. It seems driven to hypothesize about the structure of the world even in the face of evidence that no pattern exists.

These findings not only bring life to an idea we began the conversation of this book with—we are hardwired to tell stories—but they also demonstrate a companion human drive to make sense of the world, indicating that we are hardwired to make sense of the world, or to learn.

These empirical insights are also particularly helpful in beginning to understand the experience of videomaking in K-12 learning environments. Though we've certainly gotten used to the idea of how well received videomaking is by students, we still cannot help wonder truly why it is so enriching for kids, beyond the simple novelty of the experience.

The multidimensional context around the creation of youth video is certainly rich in implications involving the opportunities for youth voice, and also the creation of unique forms and processes of doing youth-based digital media storytelling. Videomaking in K-12 settings encourages and allows creative space for sense-making, and also, in Woolf's sense, small almost peripheral discoveries that come out of the narratives of sense-making.

Day in My Life

When the eighty-five students in our Smart Kids Visual Stories Project were given the chance to be seen and heard, they always had stories to tell that reflected how they made sense of the experiences of their education. To date they have produced hundreds of hours of footage, nearly three terabytes of digital video stories about their experiences and perspectives on school.

But this footage and the stories compiled from it also unearthed interesting complexities around the confabulative storytelling process students engaged in. When it comes to the storytelling process around the K-12 videomaking experience, there is no manual of how to tell a story, what kind of story it should be, what form of media or genre would fit the story best. Story is a very complicated word and when you add moving images and sound it gets even more complicated, especially as it relates to the media production process surrounding its creation. This was illustrated in recent experiences surrounding seventh grader Talia Edwards's visual story at Corrigan K-8 School.

FLASH FORWARD:
SMART KIDS VISUAL STORY #9
"A Day in My Life"
by Talia Edwards, Corrigan School, Grade 7
INTERIOR: CLASSROOM (CORRIGAN SCHOOL)—MORNING

We are looking at part of the classroom from a very odd, perhaps unintended angle as if recording something that was not meant to be recorded. Talia is partially revealed as she enters left frame with equipment bag, tripod, and small video camera in her hand. Some classmates near her are facing off-screen right in the direction of the teacher who is out of frame. We hear Talia's voice-over, describing the action.

TALIA (voiceover)
One day in my second period class I got to class late with a lot of equipment in my hands. As soon as I got settled in and had almost everything put away—except my camera which I was examining at the time—The teacher starting yelling at another student. By time she was done I was just about to put my camera away when she started yelling at me. In confusion, I turned around and just listened, just catching the angry question.

TEACHER (yelling)
Why do you have that camera in my classroom?!

TALIA (quietly)
It's for a project. At my old school this group of people from the university came to my school and we made a video of our experience. Now they're coming back to see us in our new environment.

TEACHER (yelling)
Who gave you permission to have a camera in my classroom? You need to put that away!

TALIA
The principal gave me permission.

TEACHER (yelling)
The principal can't give you permission to have something in my classroom! This is my classroom!

TALIA (voiceover)
By now I've turned around [away] in anger but didn't do or say anything.

TEACHER (yelling)
Look at me when I'm taking to you!

TALIA (voiceover)
So I turned around [to face the teacher], but she didn't say anything. Then she got up and I turned back around [away].

TEACHER (yelling)
You know what? I'm sick and tired of your behavior! Go to ISS! [In-School Suspension].

TALIA
For what? What did I do?

TALIA (voiceover)
She gave me a lot of false reasons.

TEACHER (yelling)
You can either go to ISS or you will have lunch detention!

TALIA (voiceover)
So I quietly picked up all of my stuff, and went to ISS for time out, but I ended up having to stay the whole period.

FADE TO BLACK

TALIA (voiceover)
This situation made me mad, and made me feel like I was helpless.

Context of the Project

Talia's story began in her second year with the Smart Kids Visual Stories. She was one of twenty-two students we followed after the district decided to close the original K-8 school we were based in. In the previous year, Talia was also one of eighty-five students (the number fluctuated as students entered and left during the school year) we met in the 4th, 5th, and 6th grades of the Garber School. Over the school year we engaged in media exercises with as many of the students as possible (including brief camera and editing training sessions) resulting in four different types of projects.

Why Video?

It is important to explain why this research project is framed around student-produced media—specifically video stories. We could have simply asked the students to tell us what they thought of education and transcribed it. This comes down to three factors:

- Public visibility of visual media—easily shared
- Familiarity and comparative relevance of visual media with students
- The opportunity for the university to strengthen student media skills
- Past success with visual media in inspiring student discussion and expression
- The eye of visual media in seeing in the shadows of everyday life

Scholars have found additional merits of video in student settings. Visual media like digital video are an important part of urban high school students' lives outside of school. However, "... [S]chools are arguably out of touch with the everyday literacies that many youth find relevant and into which they, in part, are socialized" (Alverman and Eakle, 2007).

Miller and Borowicz (2005) found that digital video functioned to "awaken something in students that traditional academic tools of books and paper do not." Approaches such as *photovoice* emphasize that giving people cameras to represent their lives promotes "critical group discussion about personal and community issues and assets" (Wang, Morrel-Samuels, Hutchison, Bell, and Pestronk, 2004).

Talia's Visual Story

Talia was one of six Garber students we followed to the Corrigan School. Corrigan was seen as a better school than Garber because it was in a comparatively more upscale neighborhood, closer to the university and—unlike Garber where nearly all students were bussed in from outlying neighborhoods—it was a community school where a large number of students were within easy walking distance.

When it was Talia's turn to respond to the question of what she wanted to tell a visual story about, she had no doubts.

"Racism in the classroom," she announced confidently. "My second period teacher is a racist and I want to do a story about it."

Messy Engagement: Collision of Communities

Talia's declaration was an example of one of the many flashpoints in the project that illuminated the rich complexities surrounding a seemingly simple process of collecting stories from young people.

In an ecological sense, a community is a group of interdependent organisms of different species growing or living together in a specified habitat. By bringing the intellectually driven digital storytelling project from the university community into the pedagogically driven process of public education delivery, we were setting up, not only an intersection of community interests, but also possible collisions of interests, and ultimately changes in these communities. The question is, who and what principles govern such intersections, inevitable collisions, and ultimate transformations?

Not only that, but also, where are the lines of communities and what rights do these communities possess when it comes to securing their boundaries? Certainly in a very broad sense, we were bringing communities of higher education and public education together, but "zooming in" a little closer, we were also bringing together sub-communities within, including: teachers, administrators, grade levels, cultural groups (international and racial), two very different schools of a university with different practices, values, and politics, and the broad array of unique principles, actions, and needs within these communities. And as we moved closer to the creation of stories, we also unearthed storytelling communities (fiction, nonfiction, artistic)—each with their own set of principles, values, and techniques, not to mention the differences between audiences of these stories—their expectations and needs. The fact is, all of these communities were touched in the process of making Smart Kids Visual Stories.

The Story within Talia's Story

Talia was smiling when she arrived at the main office to pick up her camera and tripod. She would be recording her "Day in My Life"—her entire school day—on the next day by herself. It was an exciting prospect to think of what she would find in the wide open world of school-based verité. Talia was a strong personality, and she really believed in her story, so we weren't worried about her. It was easier to imagine all the things she might discover with her camera in real school life.

Two days later when she arrived at the school office to return the equipment, Talia was not smiling; in fact she was completely avoiding eye contact. When asked if everything was ok, she replied, "No," handed us the camera and tripod and started walking back to her class.

Talia was obviously hurt, and we considered letting her leave and following up on the matter later, but given the fact that we were responsible for setting her up on this now venture-gone-wrong, we felt responsible for her and her well-being.

Following her down the hall on her way back to class, we discovered that the teacher Talia had been trying to tell a story about suspended her for bringing a camera into the class. The teacher told her that she had no right to bring a camera into her class even if the principal said it was OK.

We assured Talia that based on what she had told us she had done nothing wrong and apologized for the hurt this experience had caused her. We let her know that we would be talking to the principal about what happened.

"Can I leave now?" she asked, obviously still hurting from the experience.

Teacher's Rights

Enter the dialectic between teaching community and the student community. Who were we as university outsiders to support the idea of a student going into a teacher's classroom with a camera looking for incidents of racism?

Granted, the student was not proclaiming such an objective to the teacher. She was simply documenting her entire school day, part of which was her second period class with this teacher.

Regardless, was it right for us to encourage this activity knowing that the student's objective was to portray racism on the teacher's part in conducting the class? This is another instance of messy engagement that warrants careful consideration. In our minds, we were staying close to the objectives of our research project—to support students in the process of creating their visual stories. The other side of this messy equation: Is it right for us to question the student's story topic and motives behind it, and conceivably judge it as appropriate or inappropriate as a visual story? The simple answer was, "No." But this was not by any means a simple issue.

What if a student wanted to do a story about a "bad teacher?" We certainly would not want to put ourselves in the position of saying to a student who has been invited to tell the stories that must be told, "No, we're sorry you can't do that." But at the same time, we cannot ignore the fact that such a story objective may hurt both the teacher and the school it is about, placing us squarely between the interests of teachers and students.

The Teacher-Student Dimension

Early in the project, we established an environment of listening where students came to accept the idea that we would listen first. Our belief was that difficult topics could come out of an environment of trust and openness. Many times when we would be talking to the students about their lives and perspectives, we could sense the growing ease of their expression. Oftentimes, students would warn one another that they shouldn't be talking about what they were talking about because it was a dangerous topic, particularly when it came to discussions of teacher attitudes, bad behavior, and racial issues.

When Talia first mentioned doing a story on racism in the classroom, we were both proud—that she trusted us to bring up a topic that students, and teachers generally found difficult to talk about—and worried. The worry came from the cultural and political power of the word racism, considering that this African-American girl was surrounded by mostly white and privileged researchers, teachers, and administrators.

We also considered what little ground we had to stand on in this issue. Who were we to negotiate a public conversation on racism? If we stayed close to the project, assisting students in their efforts to "articulate a public voice and share insights on urban education reform in ways that are meaningful to them," then we had a great deal more ground. But within the converging communities of university, public school, and student, we faced limits. With this in mind, we talked extensively about the subject of racism and how she would like to tell the story.

Talia's Story: Concept and Genre

We began by discussing what she meant by racism and how she felt it materialized in the class. Talia explained that all the black students were in one corner of the class and all the white students in the other, and the teacher treated the two groups very differently, favoring the white kids. She also said the teacher was "very mean."

It didn't take long for Talia to decide on the *vérité* style for her story. She would employ the "day-in-my-life" technique some of the students had used in the previous year in documenting a typical day for them outside of school to help others in their class learn more about them. In Talia's case, the day in her life would be a typical school day. In order for Talia to do this, we felt it best to get permission from the principal.

The Administrative Culture

Though we knew Lori Pettine and her school very well, the air of messy engagement was coming on strong as we approached her office. Being at Corrigan was truly personal. Our own children had attended this very school. Plus, the school was no stranger to the impact of being on the periphery of a major university. Principal Pettine had been very close to the project from the beginning, holding the initial meetings between the kids and our research team in her office to make sure she understood the project and also to insure that we, as researchers, felt welcome in her school. She wanted to make sure we had the necessary resources to conduct our research.

The messiness of our engagement at Corrigan was in the fact that our work was built upon an academic protocol. Because of that, we had no intention of telling Lori that a student in our IRB-approved research study was interested in telling a visual story about the incidence of racism in one of her classrooms. Our priority was in allowing students the opportunity to express their perspectives on school experience. Revealing this story topic could conceivably put the principal in the position of blocking it. The spirit of our research project was to encourage expression, not to block it.

But that wasn't all. At the same time, we had no intention of letting a student's pursuit of a story harm the school. There would be several layers of oversight in our research process that would provide the opportunity, if necessary, to consider the harm a student-produced visual story might do to the school and/or other students. But we did not think the beginning of the project was the point to intervene.

Ironically, years ago we had witnessed an event in this very school where some very young students and the school were harmed because of a nationally broadcast new magazine exposé involving children's (out of context) views on the subject of sex. Though the major motive of our research study may have been to help students express their perspectives on education, it was not without concern for simultaneous and complex interests of teachers, administrators, and parents surrounding them.

In the meeting with Principal Pettine, we informed her that one of the six students involved in the Smart Kids Visual Stories Project wanted to bring a video camera with her to document a day in her life at school. It was important that she approved of the idea in principle and had the chance to notify the seventh grade teachers who would be affected. She not only approved the request, but also thought it was a very good idea.

Talia's Suspension

Despite her cooperation, we were not sure how Principal Pettine would react to the problem surrounding Talia's in-school suspension by her second period teacher. As soon as we saw her she shook her head and apologized, saying the teacher had overreacted. She had spoken to the teacher about the experience in a special meeting involving Talia's parents, and assured us that Talia was perfectly welcome to return to the class with the camera, and finish her project.

But when Talia was informed of the good news the next day, she explained that she was no longer interested in doing a Smart Kids story. The experience had been completely humiliating for her and she didn't want it to happen again. When she asked if she could go back to class, we seized on the opportunity to ask her if she could at least help Leia, the other 7th grader, with her project as opposed to leaving the project all together. She agreed.

Walking the Line

Talia had attempted to tell a story about racism in school and had been silenced before she could finish making it. In battling with the idea of pushing her to stay with the project, or letting her return to normal student life, we pondered whether we were doing this for our interests or hers. We were clearly walking the line of possibly harming this child if our gut feeling that she would be better telling the story somehow, some way, rather than walking away with the scar of having failed. So we decided to be patient and slowly try to work Talia back into her story once she had a little recovery time.

In the free moments around planning and shooting Leia's story, we continued talking to Talia about her unfortunate experience in shooting her day-in-the-life story, and little by little she warmed up, eventually agreeing to try her hand at a story. But she really did not want to face her second period teacher with a camera again, as that had hurt her too much.

Given the passion she had shown for her original story idea, we asked her if she would consider telling the story of what had happened to her in the class when she was suspended. She was curious about how she would do this. A good start would be for her to write down in her own words what had happened and then read it into the camera microphone as a voiceover. After that, we could talk about what kinds of pictures—moving or still—might complement the reading of the story. We decided to have Leia record Talia's voiceover in our video editing complex during one of the regularly scheduled field trips to the university. The field trips brought Smart Kids from four area schools together to talk about their stories and help each other with the creative and technological processes.

Acting like long term veterans of the editing suites, Leia and Talia went straight to their favorite room to begin their work. A few minutes later, Leia called us back into the room to look at something.

They had discovered a short recording of the actual 2nd period class where Talia had been suspended. It appeared to be an unintentional recording because the camera view was oddly tilted, with off-screen sound—apparently an adult woman shouting at someone—as if it was recorded by accident. We sat down in the editing suite and watched and listened to the inadvertent clip over and over. It was about ten seconds in total—not a lot to work with.

> VIDEO:
> "You need to put that camera away!"
> "Not in my classroom, you don't!"

Our first reaction was concern for Talia. We worried the sounds would upset her, and rekindle her anxiety, but she actually seemed confident, almost content, like she had an idea.

> VIDEO:
> "You need to put that camera away!"
> "Not in my classroom, you don't!"

We asked them what they were thinking. Leia asked if we could use the clip in Talia's story. Talia's eyes lit up. "But you can't see anything," Talia concluded.

As in just about every step in this story process, this situation presented a path of messy engagement. The TV production teacher in us saw a teachable moment, something that could be seen as us coming up with an idea for Talia's project, but regardless it rose naturally out of Talia's story process. This particular brand of messy engagement happened all the time in the college teaching environment, specifically when students were deeply involved in the creative process.

Students' creative challenges usually invited a consideration of ideas and approaches that were just outside of their own ability to comprehend on their own. We call them teaching moments because they invite an expansion of a student's existing creative process. Such moments usually involve questions like, "Have you considered this technique for your story?" or, "Is that the best shot for your story to lead with?" or "If you're trying to tell a story about 'x' wouldn't it make more sense for the story if you moved in *this* direction?" Though it involves a process of giving students other ideas, the purpose behind such creative interaction is not to do the work for the student, but rather to engage the student in a wider contemplation of storytelling process that their idea may be best served by.

When it came to Talia's story we presented the girls with such a contemplation of their story idea. What if they were to re-enact the rest of their story in a similar way that Talia actually captured those ten seconds of off-camera action, sideways framing, and accidental-recording-style real footage? This would involve laying down Talia's voice narrating the story, and inserting a reenactment of the classroom incident to fit it. They could shoot the reenactment from a tilted point of view of Talia's partial torso in reaction to a teacher yelling at her off-camera. Viewers could then get a visual sense of what was happening without disclosing a specific identity of a teacher.

Talia and Leia loved the idea, and felt comfortable taking ownership of it in relation to their story. We shot the reenactment a few days later during their lunch period and then chose some music to complement the emotional tone of her feelings about the event. We even added the actual audio from the shouting teacher and repeated the lines to reflect Talia's anger and helplessness in the story.

Messy Collaboration

Our research team regularly visualized the collaborative part of our project as something that happened *after* the students told their stories, for instance going with them to present their stories to the school board and helping them follow up on their stories as they inform best educational practices for the future. But in Talia's case, we were clearly collaborating within the process of her expression of the story.

Was this truly Talia's story, if we helped her? In the hours and hours we had spent with the Smart Kids, we had helped some of them a lot, and others, not at all. It depended on the story and the child telling it. Were the stories we helped them with better or more presentable than the ones we had not? Not necessarily, but the fact remains that the process was not neat and clean—rather parallel to the messiness that storytellers must deal with. Virginia Woolf (1925) advised storytellers to trace the pattern of their expressions "however disconnected and incoherent in appearance." This is something our minds, in Michael Gazanniga's work (2012), are conditioned to do every day:

> Our subjective awareness arises out of our dominant left hemisphere's unrelenting quest to explain the bits and pieces that pop into consciousness. What does it mean that we build our theories about ourselves after the fact? How much of the time are we confabulating, giving a fictitious account of a past event, believing it to be true? When thinking about these big questions, one must always remember that all these modules are mental systems selected for over the course of evolution. The individuals who possessed them made choices that resulted in survival and reproduction. They became our ancestors.

The messiness we were experiencing in our particular storytelling process was in fact an exercise of a naturally human sense-making process. In the end, we determined that our success would depend on the extent to which students took ownership of their stories.

Conclusion

[S]chools need to think hard about how they should respond to the more participatory forms of media culture that are now emerging. . . .
—David Buckingham in Youth, Identity, and Digital Media

We saw Talia when we delivered her Smart Kids movie poster announcing their premiere date and time. She looked very happy and proud at the prospect of the upcoming event in her honor. She asked if she had to dress up and seemed pleased when we told her, "Of course you do. It's a movie premiere!"

A new challenge had emerged: what dress would she wear for such an affair? It had not been that long ago when we were looking at a defeated and humiliated version of Talia surrendering her camera and announcing she would no longer be part of the Smart Kids project. At this point it felt like we had done the right thing, to push Talia to continue with her project, and we couldn't help but feel a tinge of relief—all this at a point weeks before her project would be formally, publically listened to.

This exchange confirmed to us how important the first step of the story process is in the goal of capturing student stories and perspectives on education, or more broadly the power and strength of exercising personal expression through media.

Yes, there was certainly more to gain (or conceivably lose) in the public screening of the stories: the listening phase of the storytelling process. But there was already a sign of real success here in the first phase—expression—along with a deep well of possibilities to explore in future research projects.

We held a Hollywood-style movie premiere—complete with red carpet—of the ten Smart Kids Visual Stories at our large university auditorium filled with friends, family members, and other fans of the Smart Kids.

As long as the projector doesn't break, or the power doesn't go out, such events are as a rule very neat and clean and enjoyable for those involved. The Smart Kids premiere was certainly no exception.

But behind the façade, those involved in the story process will know how messy it was to make these stories. From the process of negotiating with the schools, to the closing of a school to the following of as many of the original students as we could, to the enormously complex parental permission process, to the even more complicated transportation process to get middle school kids to the university (not to mention back home after that), to the training sessions, to the lapses in time—sometimes days, weeks, or months between our time together—and through it all these kids were turning into young adults before our eyes.

As the account of Talia's story process demonstrates, at just about every turn, considering young people in urban school environments as qualified authors of media content involves far more than simply placing instruments of production in their hands, or asking them to tell a visual story.

Telling a visual story in a school environment involves careful thought, hard work, tough choices, and nearly constant uncertainty—in short, a messy process that most schools are not yet equipped to handle. Does this deem K-12 videomaking unadvisable? Based on this and every other visual story these students created—absolutely not. Why is this?

Despite the fact that kids in urban schools are often characterized as not caring about doing well in school (Alonso et al., 2009), the young storytellers we worked with demonstrated a consistent passion to do well in school and saw their successful education as a vital part of their futures.

These Smart Kids truly enjoyed the experience of telling stories for others to hear. It made them feel important and respected. And as far as their telling of these stories goes, schools and the process of education are messy, so why wouldn't the stories around them be similarly messy: messy questions involve messy answers.

Kids enjoy talking about education not only because it is very important to them but also because they enjoy the experience of expressing their ideas about the world in general. Expressing through video stories empowered Talia and the other Smart Kids. Our work with them only scratched the surface as far as opening up their channels of expression. We—researchers, teachers, public school administrators—need to invite more stories from children and prepare ourselves to listen to them.

As David Buckingham (2009) advises above, and others back up from various points of view (Alvermann and Eakle, 2007; Burke and Burke, 2005; Burke and Grosvenor, 2003; Cook-Sather, 2002; Cushman and the Students of What Kids Can Do, 2003), the evolving media landscape poses a frontier of sorts for student expressions. Based on the Smart Kids project, some aspects of expression are familiar, and others, Talia's story for instance, are potentially inventive. Such expressions seem worthy of a genre of their own.

The production process is rich with story content and meaning, certainly giving credence to calls for looking as closely at the periphery of visual stories (Rose, 2007) as at the stories themselves: in other words, the stories are not the whole story. But also, transcending Rose's largely still picture methodology, when pictures move and contain sounds, their richness increases exponentially.

Change is hard: both changes that are intended, university-school partnerships to seek student perspectives on education, and changes that are not, like people getting hurt and offended along the way.

And finally, returning to the question of why? Why do kids of all ages and grade levels so consistently light up when movie cameras enter their worlds, especially classrooms? Beyond the novelty, beyond the technological gadgetry with all of its resident complications there is clearly a deeper, more meaningful force at work. Perhaps the most important key to unlocking the moviemaking mind is understanding that we are all living, breathing, confabulating stories in the making. The process around our living involves making sense of those stories, telling those stories, aspiring to the expectations of those stories and embodying those stories as they slowly bring to view a dynamic image of our sense of the world we live in and who we are as characters in that world. A camera provides one conduit, among many, for these stories: stories that will not only show the world who we are and what we are about, but more importantly, in the same way show ourselves.

References

Adams, Marilyn Jager. (1990). *Beginning to Read: Thinking and Learning about Print.* Urbana-Champaign: University of Illinois, Reading Research and Education Center.

Agency. (2013). In *Merriam-Webster.com.* Retrieved from: http://www.merriam-webster.com/dictionary/agency.

Alonso, Anderson, Su, & Theoharis (2009). *Our Schools Suck: Students Talk Back to a Segregated Nation on the Failures of Urban Education.* NY: NYU Press.

Alvermann, D., and Eakle, J. (2007). Dissolving Learning Boundaries: The Doing, Redoing, and Undoing of School. In D. Thiessen and A. Cook-Sather (eds.), *International Handbook of Student Experience in Elementary and Secondary School* (pp. 143–66). Dordrecht, The Netherlands: Springer.

Arnone, M. P. (2005). *Motivational Design: The Secret to Producing Effective Children's Media.* Lanham, MD: Scarecrow Press.

Barker, C. (2011). *Cultural Studies: Theory and Practice* (4th ed.). Thousand Oaks, CA: Sage.

Bauerlein, M. (2011, July 07). [Web log message]. Retrieved from http://chronicle.com/blogs/brainstorm/critical-thinking-in-the-curriculum-donald-lazere/37094.

Bawarshi, Anis. "The Ecology of Genre." Ecocomposition: Theoretical and Pedagogical Approaches. Eds. Christian R. Weisser and Sydney I. Dobrin. Albany: SUNY Press, 2001. 69–80.

Bazerman, C., Bonini, A. and Figueiredo D., eds. (2009). *Genre in a Changing World.* Fort Collins, CO: The WAC Clearinghouse and Parlor Press.

Bruner, J. and Weisser, S. (1991). "The Invention of Self: Autobiography and Its Forms." In D. R. Olson & N. Torrance (Eds.), *Literacy and Orality.* Cambridge: Cambridge University Press.

Buckingham, D. (1993a). *Children Talking Television: The Making of Television Literacy.* Basingstoke, England: Falmer Press.

Buckingham, D. (ed.). (1993b). *Reading Audiences: Young People and the Media.* Manchester: Manchester University Press.

Buckingham, D. (2000). *After the Death of Childhood: Growing Up in the Age of Electronic Media.* Cambridge, UK: Polity Press.

Buckingham, D. (ed.). (2002). "Introduction: The Child and the Screen" in *Small Screens: Television for Children.* London and New York: Leicester University Press.

Buckingham, D. (2008). "Introducing Identity." *Youth, Identity, and Digital Media.* Edited by David Buckingham. The John D. and Catherine T. MacArthur Foundation Series on Digital Media and Learning. Cambridge, MA: The MIT Press, 2008. 1–24.

Burke, C., and Burke, W. (2005). "Student-ready Schools." *Childhood Education,* 81:5, 281–85.

Burke, C., and Grosvenor, I. (2003). *The School I'd Like: Children's and Young People's Reflections on Education for the 21st Century.* London: Routledge Falmer.

Centre for Educational Research and Education (CERI). (2007). *Understanding the Brain, The Birth Of A Learning Science.* Paris: Oecd Publishing.

Clark, R., and Salomon, G. (1986). "Media in Teaching." In M. C. Wittrock (Ed.) *Handbook of Research on Teaching* (3rd ed., pp. 464–78). NY: Macmillan.

Cohen, I. B. (1985). *Revolution in Science.* Cambridge, MA: Harvard University Press.

Cook-Sather, A. (2002). *Authorizing Students' Perspectives: Toward Trust, Dialogue, and Change in Education.* Educational Researcher, 31(4) 3–14.

Cushman, K., and the Students of What Kids Can Do. (2003). *Fires in the Bathroom: Advice for Teachers from High School Students*. New York: The New York Press.

Devlin, K. J. (2011). *Mathematics Education for a New Era: Video Games as a Medium for Learning*. Natick, MA: A. K. Peters, Ltd.

Gardner, H. (1983). *Frames Of Mind: The Theory of Multiple Intelligences*. New York: Basic Books.

Gauntlett, D. (1996). *Video Critical: Children, The Environment and Media Power*. Luton: John Libbey Media.

Gazzaniga, M. (2012). http://discovermagazine.com/2012/brain/22-interpreter-in-your-head-spins-stories.

Gazzaniga, M. (2005). The ethical brain. New York: Dana Press.

Gordon, Edwin E. (1990). *A Music Learning Theory for Newborn and Young Children*. Chicago: GIA Publications.

Gross, L. (1974). "Symbolic Competence." In D. R. Olson (Ed.). *Media and Symbols: The Forms of Expression, Communication, and Education*. The National Society for the Study of Education: Chicago.

Hays, Charlotte. "Angela Duckworth talks to IC, *In Character*. Grit: Spring 2009. http://incharacter.org/features/angela-duckworth-talks-to-ic/.

Hobbs, R. (1998). *The Seven Great Debates in the Media Literacy Movement*. Journal of Communication, 48(1):16–32.

Hobbs, R. (2007). *Reading the Media, Media Literacy in High School English*. Teachers College Press.

Kaba, Mariame. (2001). "They Listen to Me … But They Don't Act On It." In *The High School Journal*. Vol. 84, No. 2 (Dec. 2000–Jan. 2001), pp. 21–34.

Krulwich, R. (2001) *Virginia Woolf, at the intersection of Scienc and Art*. NPR Weekend Edition. July 15, 2011.http://www.npr.org/player/v2/mediaPlayer.html?action=1&t=1&islist=false&id=93184407&m=93218243.

Lehrer, J. (2007). *Proust Was a Neuroscientist*. New York: Houghton Mifflin Harcourt.

Lloyd-Kolkin, Donna, and Kathleen R. Tyner. (1991). *Media & You: An Elementary Media Literacy Curriculum*. Englewood Cliffs, NJ: Educational Technology Publications.

Longstaff, P. H., Velu, R., and Obar, J. (2004, June). *Resilience for Industries in Unpredictable Environments: You Ought To Be Like Movies*. Retrieved from http://www.pirp.harvard.edu/pubs_pdf/longsta/longsta-p04-1.pdf.

Lubbock, Sir John. (1889). *The Pleasures of Life*. London: Macmillan and Co. Presented by Authorama: Public Domain Books. http://www.authorama.com/pleasures-of-life-13.html.

Lumet, S. (1995). *Making Movies*. New York: Alfred A. Knopf, Inc.

Manu, K. (2008). Productive Failure. *Cognition and Instruction*, 26(3), 379–424.

Manu, K., & Kinzer, C. K. (2009). Productive failure in CSCL Groups. *International Journal of Computer-Supported Collaborative Learning*, 4(1), 21–46.

Marvin, C. (1988). *When Old Technologies Were New*. New York: Oxford University Press.

McCloud, S. (1993). *Understanding Comics: The Invisible Art*. New York: Harper Collins.

McEachern, W. A. (2012). *Economics: A Contemporary Introduction* (9th ed.). Mason, OH: South-Western Cengage Learning.

McIntyre, A. (2000). "Constructing Meaning About Violence, School, and Community: Participatory Action Research With Urban Youth." *The Urban Review* 32(2), 123–54.

McLuhan, M. (1994). *Understanding media: The extensions of man*. Boston, MA: The MIT Press (Original work published 1964).

Meaney, M (2001) *Nature, Nurture, and the Disunity of Knowledge*. Annals of the New York Academy of Sciences 935:50–61.

Miller, S. and Borowicz, S. (2005). "City Voices, City Visions: Digital Video as aLiteracy/Learning Supertool in Urban Classrooms." In L. Johnson, M. Finn, and R. Lewis (Eds.) *Urban Education with an Attitude*. Albany: State University of New York Press.

Navas, Eduardo. "Electronic Literature and the Mashup of Analog and Digital Code." dichtung-digital 40 (2010). http://www.dichtung-digital.org/2010/navas.htm. Accessed January 6, 2013.

Norton, Donna. (1983). *Through the Eyes of a Child.* Columbus, OH: Charles E. Merrill Publishing Co.

Olson, D. R. (Ed.) (1974). *Media and Symbols: The Forms of Expression, Communication, and Education.* The National Society for the Study of Education: Chicago.

Olson D. R., Hildyard, A., and Torrance N. (1985). *Literacy, Language and Learning: The Nature and Consequences of Reading and Writing.* Cambridge University Press.

Olson, D. R. (1987). "Schooling and the Transformation of Common Sense." in F. van Holthoon, and D. R. Olson (Eds.), *Common Sense: The Foundations for Social Science.* Lanham, MD: University Press of America, 319–40.

Olson, D. R. (Ed.) (1994). *The World on Paper: The Conceptual and Cognitive Implications of Writing and Reading.* Cambridge: Cambridge University Press.

Prensky, Marc. (2001). *Digital Game-Based Learning.* New York: McGraw Hill.

Rich, M., S. Lamola, et. al. (2000). *Asthma in the Life Context: Video Intervention/Prevention Assessment (VIA).* Pediatrics 105 (3 Pt 1): 469–77.

Rich, M. (2004). *Health Literacy via Media Literacy: Video Intervention/Prevention Assessment. American Behavioral Scientist* 48(48), 165–88.

Rich, M. (2012, March 8). *Video Intervention/Prevention Assessment.* Retrieved from http://www.cmch.tv/via/aboutus/default.asp.

Riddle, J. (2009). *Engaging the Eye Generation: Visual Literacy Strategies for the K-5 Classroom.* Portland, ME: Stenhouse Publishers.

Schoonmaker, M. (2007). *Cameras in the Classroom.* Lanham, MD: Rowman and Littlefield Education.

Schulkind, J. (ed.). (1978). "A Sketch of the Past" from *Moments of Being: Unpublished Autobiographical Writings* [Virginia Woolf]. New York: Harcourt Brace Jovanovich.

Sefton-Green, Julian (ed.). (1999). *Young People, Creativity and New Technologies: The Challenge of Digital Arts.* London and New York: Routledge.

Selfe, Cynthia L. (1999). *Technology and Literacy in the Twenty-First Century: The Importance of Paying Attention.* Carbondale and Edwardsville: Southern Illinois University Press.

Smyth, J., and McInerney, P. (2007). *Teachers in the Middle: Reclaiming the Wasteland of Adolescent Years of Schooling.* New York: Peter Lang.

Sylwester, R., and Marcinkiewicz H., (2003) *The Brain, Technology, and Education: An Interview with Robert Sylweste*r. Originally published in The Technology Source (http://ts.mivu.org/) November/December 2003. Current URL: http://technologysource.org/article/brain_technology_and_education/.

Sylwester, R. (1995). *A Celebration of Neurons: An Educator's Guide to the Human Brain.* Alexandria, VA: Association for Supervision and Curriculum Development.

Sylwester, R. (2003). *The Brain, Technology, and Education: An Interview with Robert Sylwester* by Henryk Marcinkiewicz and Robert Sylwester.

Tyner, K. (1994). "Video in the Classroom: A Tool for Reform." In *Arts Education Policy Review* Vol. 96, No. 1, September/October 1994.

Tyner, K. (1995). "Re: Jo Holz presentation." Online posting. 29 September 1995. Media-l. 29 September 1995. media-l@nmsu.edu.

Tyner, K. (1998). *Literacy in a Digital World: Teaching and Learning in the Age of Information.* Mahwah, NJ: Lawrence Erlbaum Associates, Publishers.

Using Inventive Spelling. (2005). LinguaLinks Library, Version 4.0, CD-ROM. 16 March 1999, from SIL International, at: www.sil.org/lingualinks/literacy/ImplementALiteracyProgram/UsingInventiveSpelling.htm (accessed 9 April 2005).

Wang, C., Morrel-Samuels, S., Hutchison, P., Bell, L., and Pestronk, R. (2004). Flint Photovoice: Community Building Among Youths, Adults and Policymakers. *American Journal of Public Health* 94(6), 911–13.

West, M. (1997). *Trust Your Children: Voices Against Censorship in Children's Literature,* 2nd ed. New York: Newl-Schuman Publishers, Inc.

Wise, T. (2011). *White Like Me: Reflections On Race From Privileged Son* (Revised and Updated Edition). Berkeley, CA: Soft Skull Press.
Woolf, Virginia (1925). *The Common Reader*. New York: Harcourt, Inc.

CPSIA information can be obtained at www.ICGtesting.com
Printed in the USA
BVOW03*1608120114

341559BV00002B/5/P